PLEASE, SPELL THE NAME RIGHT

PLEASE, SPELL THE NAME RIGHT

Jed Allan

with Rusty Fischer

McKenna Publishing Group
Indian Wells, California

Please, Spell the Name Right

ISBN: 1-932172-20-3
LCCN: 2004106857

Cover design by Leslie Parker

First Edition
10 9 8 7 6 5 4 3 2 1
Printed in the United States of America

Visit us on the Web at: www.mckennapubgrp.com

Dedication

To Toby, who gave me her heart, her soul, and her laughter for forty-three years of marriage. Who tried to instill in me, and everyone she met, the joy of living. I love you and miss you still.

To my sons, Rick, Dean, and Mitch. Without them I could have never made the adjustment.

To my daughters-in-law, who are my daughters.

And to Alexis, Jake, Nick, Kaytie, Rachel, and Hannah who I will love and adore forever.

Contents

Prologue: *(Not Quite) Six Feet Under*..................9

The 50s: *Innocence Lost*..................17

The 60s: *Be Our Guest*..................53

The 70s: *Night Owl*..................119

The 80s: *Daytime's Leading Man*..................155

The 90s: *Fame Has a New Zip Code*..................179

2001: *Goodbye, Dearest One*..................193

Epilogue: *The Kids are All Right*..................199

PROLOGUE:

(Not Quite) Six Feet Under

"Kathy *Bates*?" I ask into the cordless phone, pacing the length of my living room nervously as the lawn crew outside makes unintentional topiaries out of my prize hedgerows. "I'm flattered, Joanne, but why would I wanna drive all the way down there and read in front of another actress?"

It's late afternoon in sunny Palm Springs and my agent, Joanne Halpern, is eager to set up another "must do" guest appearance on another one of what she refers to as, "the next big thing."

God bless her. With Joanne, it's *always* the next big thing. But I gotta admit, she's been right so far. From *Silk Stalkings* to *Walker: Texas Ranger*, together we've been keeping my face out there—and those residuals coming in. Still, it takes a lot to get me to go to LA these days. And auditioning for fellow actors isn't one of them. "Do I really have to read, Jo? I mean, come on already. Can't we just send them a reel?"

"I know, I know," Joanne commiserates as she kicks it up a notch into "mother hen" mode. I picture her speaking into one of those newfangled headgear phone thingies, like the kids wear at McDonald's these days, smacking gum and passing over twelve headshots as she goes through the motions as a personal favor to me. "Ten years ago, nobody of your stature had to read. Five years ago, even. Today, *everybody* reads. You're not alone, Jed, this much we both know."

I'm with her there. Be it ego, job security, or perhaps a little bit of both, the days of "sending over" your next head shot and assuming it's a "sure thing" have gone the way of silent movies and contract stars. Well, for most of us anyway. Even Oscar winners and old guard Hollywood royalty are falling prey to the "younging up"—or is it "aging down"—of Tinsel Town.

As Joanne reels off the admittedly impressive roster of guest stars already signed on for this supposedly "hot, new, with it, fresh, young, cutting edge, happening" cable TV series, I grin over the oft-repeated Hollywood legend about the time Shelley Winters was asked to read by some snot-nosed young producer.

Shelley goddamn Winters, of all people.

Legend has it that Shelley, ever the old trooper, reluctantly agreed to read for whatever long forgotten part she'd been offered by, I'm quite sure, some long forgotten agent. But come the diva's short-lived audition, she plunked down her surprisingly heavy handbag, pulled her first Oscar out and, with a WHAM! that could be heard all the way to Beverly Hills, slammed it down on the casting table.

WHAM!

Out came the second of her two Best Supporting Actress Oscars.

"Now," the feisty grand dame of old guard Hollywood was reputed as asking of those peach fuzzed producers assembled before her, "Which one of you punks still wants me to read for them?"

She got the part …

Apparently, it wasn't going to be so easy for me.

"Come on, Joanne," I sigh, picturing the long drive down, the inevitably awkward "meet and greet," the nervousness, the uncertainty, the endless waiting for the call back that, admittedly, might never come. "That's gonna be pretty damn embarrassing for me, driving all the way down there to read for a guest shot. How many scenes did you say I was in again?"

"*Scenes?*" she blurts, as if I'm asking for final cut or, perhaps, two percent on the back end or something. "Try *lines*. And it's four, actually. Four lines, Jed. Four lines on what HBO promises to be the next *Sopranos*. Could be just the thing you need to stir things up, if you know what I mean."

"Four lines," I frown, staring at the carpet. "Four frickin' lines? Is it really worth it? Honestly, Jo, between you and me and the wallpaper. Waddya think? Is it that big a deal?"

"Well," she stalls expertly, bringing out the big guns in order to sway my vote in her direction, "supposedly it's an episode near and dear to the creator's heart. Alan Ball himself has written the script and, with Kathy Bates directing, I assumed it was something you were interested in doing…"

She lets it sit there, dangling the hook like the pro that she is …

"Alan Ball?" I cluck. "Now that's a different story. What are you holding *that* back for?"

The creator of *American Beauty* is attached to this project and she's pushing Kathy Bates? What's wrong with this picture?

And, more importantly, what the hell do they want with *me*?

"They're looking for someone established, someone professorial, someone *wise*," explains Joanne, pitching me the character of Dr. Garrett Feinberg for Episode 10 of the inaugural season of an upstart new cable series tentatively titled … now … what was that name again? She'd just said it a minute ago. Five Doors Down? Nope, that's not it. Seven Miles Wide? No, no …

Six Feet Under.

That's it …

"What's with the title?" I joke, already flipping through my day planner, pen in hand, and picturing the big, fat smile on my agent's face. "Somebody work in a funeral home or something?"

"Actually," explains Joanne, giving me the schpiel …

"All right, all right," I sigh one last time as Joanne reels off a date, place, and time one week hence for the audition. "God I hope this is worth it," I joke.

I hang up the phone after haggling over a few details, pace awhile, then pace some more. Four measly lines. Forty-five years in this business and I've gotta drive three hours to read less than a handful of lines? I just know I'm gonna look like some kind of a schmuck if I drive three hours to read for Kathy Bates and Alan Ball, and then … *don't* get the part!

Six days later, nervous as hell, I'm cruising from Palm Springs to LA. The scene? Who the hell knows? Some crazy broad on the show has a brother who's equally disturbed and, apparently, takes pictures. The "artsy" kind. You know. Black and white. Nudes. Bowls of fruit. That type of thing. I'm his rarely seen therapist who comes to a gallery opening and meets his sister for the very first time.

"I've heard a lot about you," I'm supposed to say when we finally meet. "And everything they say is true…

"Four lines. Four bloody lines. Screw it," I blurt to the bumper to bumper traffic outside my bug-splattered windshield. "I feel like enough of an idiot as it is. I'll just have to wing it."

Just past Fox and KTLA studios on Hollywood & Vine, I take Vine Street south for two blocks until I finally get to fabled Sunset Boulevard. Turning left, I go three more blocks until the adobe walls and looming sound stages of a typical LA movie studio tell me I'm at least getting reasonably warm.

Sunset-Gower Studios is aptly named, I think, as I cruise to the instantly recognizable corner of Sunset Boulevard and Gower Street. Or should I say, aptly *re*-named. Built in 1921, this large Hollywood movie studio was originally the historic Columbia Pictures Studios lot. It's located right in the heart of "Gower Gulch," as it's known locally, just near the corner of Gower Street and Sunset Boulevard, thus the new name.

Founded by Harry and Jack Cohn in 1920, Columbia Pictures produced a heady mixture of such instantly recognizable, mass produced B-movies as the *Three Stooges* and such classic feature films as Frank Capra's *Mr. Smith Goes to Washington*, all of them on this very lot.

While its competitor, MGM, was known as a "star's studio," most of the stars at Columbia were really just on loan from other studios. In fact, legend has it that when MGM wanted to "punish" one of its actors for one reason or another, they used to "loan" their stars to Columbia.

Local lore has it that, in one instance, the honchos at MGM thought they were "punishing" a young, upstart actor named Clark Gable when they banished him to Columbia Studios to make a "minor picture" called *It Happened One Night*. The rest, as they say, is history and Gable became a star mostly thanks to his "banishment."

The studio branched out into TV production in later years, including such 60s classics as *I Dream of Jeannie, The Flying Nun,* and *Bewitched,* but eventually Columbia was bought by Sony Entertainment, setting up shop at their current address.

Sunset-Gower's primary product is now TV shows, hence the reason I'm auditioning for a new cable series set in a funeral home, of all places, for an actress-turned-director who rose to stardom smashing both of James Caan's feet sideways with a sledgehammer and a screenwriter-turned-producer who made his name killing off Kevin Spacey with a German Lugar.

Ah, Hollywood.

My kind of town …

How do I know all of this fascinating Tinsel Town trivia? Because my agent Joanne told me so? Because I'm a closet fan of old Hollywood lore? No, I'm suddenly an expert on various movie studios in and around "Gower Gulch" because I haven't been there in so long I needed the Internet just to get directions to the place!

Flashing my smile at the gate, not to mention a photo I. D., I reel off my name like some stargazing extra and am given the go-ahead by a fresh-faced young guard (read "actor trying to get in through the front gate, quiet literally") as spiffily attired as he is dreadfully bored.

I steer my fancy car, my one and only vice, through racks of glitzy costumes and oversized props until I get to Studio 6–D and park alongside a long line of identical luxury cars, wondering idly which one belongs to Kathy Bates?

The production office isn't hard to find for an old pro like me, and after following a trail of 8 x 11 glossies and the wafting smell of raw ambition, I wind up in a room full of ten other people, all eleven of us making nice as we swap a few well-meaning rounds of "I loved you in…"

And, "You were great in …"

And, my all-time favorite, "When are you coming back on …?" God, if I never hear that one again it'll be too soon. Half the time I just want to scream, "They don't WANT me back on!"

Meanwhile, Kathy and Allan sit at a glorified picnic table surrounded by various producers, casting agents, and hangers on, all of them younger, hungrier, and with *lots* more to lose if this series should turn out to be not quite so hip, happening, cutting edge, and smart as my agent thinks it should be.

Some readings, *you're* the one in control. You're in the zone, pulling out the stops and wowing them with the same stunts you've been pulling for over four decades now. The "aw shucks" grin. The "smoldering glare."

Put me on a set with Deidre Hall or Robin Wright Penn, for instance, and I'm right at home trading box scores with the grips and flirting with the interns. Get me in a room with some of Hollywood's elite and ask me to read four awkward lines for them, however, and even *I'm* a little out of my element.

Well, that's not entirely true, either. The fact is, I'm never *really* out of my element. If I was, what kind of an actor would I be? The truth of the matter is that in most of these situations, you're totally wrong for the part. You know it. The casting director knows it.

The only one who *doesn't* know it is your agent!

So you drive for three hours feeling like a schmuck with your four piddly lines taped to the dashboard only to be told, "We'll be in touch." So why am I here today? More than likely, it's because this crew is on a deadline and needs somebody, anybody, to fill a part.

Problem is, they just don't know *who* they want.

More precisely, they don't know *what* they want …

So here I am, going through the motions, 99.9 % sure I'm not right for the part. And whenever I think there's gonna be a problem, whenever I think I've gone out of my way to make the effort only to be shot in the foot two steps through the door, my first instinct is to go for the laughs.

"We just want to thank you so much for coming down to read for such a small part," Kathy says by way of introduction, unknowingly giving me just the segue I need.

"Well, you're right," I reply, flashing my trademark smile and piling on the charm as they patiently wait for me to read those four little lines and turn back around, "it *is* a small part. And I just spent three hours stuck in traffic to get here and read them for you. That should give you some indication of how eager I am to work with you two. So I feel that, in turn, you're in some way *obligated* to me and, therefore, I will assume that I have the part …"

The laughter followed.

The ploy worked.

After that, it only took *one* line.

"I've heard a **lot** about you …"

I got the part.

The rest, as they say, is showbiz history.

Then again, I like to think, so am I …

The 50s:
All the World's a Stage

Like so many other actors, my story begins with a simple slip of paper. No, not some autograph I'd signed for a loyal fan or a love letter penned to a looming starlet or a hot script or even, for that matter, a big studio contract with MGM or Columbia.

My story starts with the year I got that little slip of paper known as my … Equity Card.

That year was 1956 …

Unemployment was just over four percent and the average house went for $22,000, though the average income was only $4,454—*before* taxes. Bread was eighteen cents, but a stamp was only three. You could get spareribs for thirty-nine cents a pound, a dozen eggs for forty-five cents, and a six-pack of Rheingold Beer for a whopping $1.20.

Harry Belafonte had the top album that year with *Calypso*, while Elvis followed closely behind with his self-titled album *Elvis Presley*. Elsewhere on the radio, you could hear Dean Martin crooning "Memories Are Made of This," Little Richard wailing "Tutti Frutti" and The Platters whining "Great Pretender."

A new breath mint was introduced, the first in candy form.

It was called … "Certs."

My Fair Lady opened at the Mark Hellinger Theatre in New York. The original production featured Rex Harrison as "Henry Higgins" and Julie Andrews as "Eliza" and enjoyed a run of nearly 2,500 performances that lasted almost a decade. I think I saw at least half of them.

Please, Spell the Name Right

The $64,000 Question, I Love Lucy, and *The Ed Sullivan Show* took the top three spots in TV ratings and Americans got their first taste of Dorothy and those little red slippers when *The Wizard of Oz* first aired on national television. On the opposite end of the spectrum, the racy and controversial bestselling book *Peyton Place* was published that same year.

Marilyn Monroe married Arthur Miller and actress Grace Kelly married Prince Rainier III of Monaco and my mother staunchly predicted that neither one would last. In a way, she was right about both. Bob Cousy, a basketball star, Bobby Lane, a football hero, and Duke Snider, from the world of baseball, all get their own Wheaties boxes.

And me?

I became what was known as "a professional actor."

(Though definitely not a "working" one …)

Then, as now, an actor couldn't work in the theater—well, not *legally* anyway—without his all-important Equity card. To get one in those days, you had to work in summer theater as an apprentice for twelve consecutive weeks—or play in at least eight shows while you were there. My how times have changed. It would be almost impossible for modern actors to achieve such a feat, given the overabundance of budding stars—and the under abundance of live performances in which to showcase themselves.

But although televisions were creeping into the living rooms of 50s families everywhere by then, theaters were still the proverbial 300-pound gorilla all across the country. Though this would shortly change, the stringent Equity requirements of twelve weeks or eight shows are a direct reflection of this current trend.

Like many budding actors in the mid-50s, I desperately wanted to be in "the business." To what extent I was not yet sure, but the desire was certainly there and had been for as long as I could remember. Perhaps it was in my blood from the very beginning. My father, in fact, was a talented musician who made a name for himself in the heyday of the swing era.

He was a killer "reed man" known for his sax, clarinet, and flute playing. (He was also a helluva singer, or "crooner" as they were termed in their day.) As the big band sound captured the hearts, and ears, of the country in the 40s and early 50s, he toured with such great orchestra leaders of the day as Woody Herman, Benny Goodman, Glen Miller, Paul Whiteman, and Larry Clinton.

Years later, as he tired of being on the road so much and wanted to be closer to home and spend time with his young family, he made the switch to Broadway, where he played with the orchestra in the recessed portion of the theater in front of the stage known as "the pit."

(Or, as he often referred to it, "the pits.")

The mid-50s found me still toiling away at American University in Washington, DC. Though I would eventually graduate with a communications degree in 1955, the theater was what appealed to me the most. While I dabbled in onstage productions for the drama department at American U, I also moonlighted at a local DC radio station called WCOP.

Already, radio's days were numbered, as we knew it, but the popular form of entertainment still had a few tricks up its sleeves as the 1950s officially reached the halfway mark. This was not to be confused with today's glory-seeking shock jocks or pie-eating contests. WNEW, where my father worked for fifteen years was still going strong in New York. My dad was playing music on the last live music station in the country. WNEW, of "Make Believe Ballroom" fame, led by disc jockeys Martin Block and William B. Williams was an incredible place to work. My father ended up his, and WNEW's tenure, working with the Teddy Wilson Quartet and Teddy Wilson, of the original Benny Goodman band.

My job at WCOP was somewhat less glamorous, however. Instead of talking or crooning, I was cleaning. The station manager graciously let me swab the decks a few days a week in exchange for pizza and beer money and, unbeknownst to him, the chance to learn from one of the masters himself.

Though a mop and a bucket were my only tools of the trade at this point, I had more than just a steady paycheck on my mind. A radio legend of some repute at that time named Gene Claven worked there. Soon to become famous for his popular show Claven & Finch, the man was already a radio legend and I was eager to do anything just to get my shot at radio stardom under his expert tutelage.

What I got instead was a swift kick in the ass …

Please, Spell the Name Right

Like many silver tongued devils of my day, I had planned on becoming a disc jockey after graduation, figuring my "mellifluous" voice, I *really* love the sound of my own voice, would find a welcome home on the airwaves. But what did I know? I was so cocky, I loved me a lot.

But one night as I took a break from mopping to swap drama department war stories with the king of silver tongues himself, Claven bluntly told me in the words I'll never forget, "Forget about disc jockeying, kid, it'll never work out. Your voice has too much New York City in it. It'll never play in Peoria ..."

I didn't want to work in Peoria anyway ...

Momentarily crushed, I turned my focus elsewhere, as I was often want to do in the face of bad news, bad advice, or bad career choices. Continuing to seek out a role model as I stretched my own wings while I was away at school, I had found a mentor in Jack Yokem, my college drama coach.

Cast my final semester in a campus production of *Detective Story*, written by Sidney Kingsley, Jack really let me shine playing a role that was true to my heart and, I must confess, just a little too easy to sink my teeth into: Charlie Genini, the crazy killer. The role had originally been played by Joseph Weismann in the gritty crime drama that had become a popular 1951 movie starring Kirk Douglas and Eleanor Parker, and in it I earned my first rave reviews, or "notices," as they were called in the theater.

More than just my drama coach, however, Jack Yokem was the first person ever to tell me I could be ... an *actor*.

Ann Bancroft was the second. Back then, of course, she was also known as Ann Italiano and her sister, Kitty Italiano, was cast in the play as well. Ms. Bancroft was not yet the star she was to become, but still well-known. After one performance, Ann came backstage to congratulate her little sister—and found me instead. "Is this what you really want to do?" she asked me, puffing away on a trademark cigarette as around us swirled the jubilant antics of a post-show celebration.

"Absolutely," I grinned, the sound of applause still ringing in my ears.

She nodded knowingly, a plume of smoke framing her head like a wreath. "Then stick with it..." was her short, but sage, advice.

Jed Allan

Since I'd always been lucky with the ladies, I eagerly took Ann's advice over Gene Claven's. Before getting my Associates of Art Degree later that year, I applied and was finally accepted to the famed Pasadena Playhouse in sunny California starting in the following September.

Things were falling into place, my life was starting to take shape …

Founded in 1917, The Pasadena Playhouse has since made an indelible mark on the American theatre. During its first four decades, The Pasadena Playhouse produced hundreds of plays, presented 477 world premieres, and was the first American theatre to present all thirty-seven of Shakespeare's plays.

Its College of Theatre Arts, known during the 1930s, 40s, and 50s as "Hollywood's talent factory," launched the careers of countless playwrights, directors, and actors such as William Holden, Gloria Stuart, Gene Hackman, and Dustin Hoffman, who had graduated the year before I arrived.

In between learning to act, sing, dance and even fence during my "penance in Pasadena," I also performed in such plays as "Two Adams for Eve" and "Accidentally Yours." But before my two years were officially up at "Hollywood's talent factory," I got an opportunity that would change my life.

Usually when my dad called me, it was to ride my ass or, more often than not, complain about sending me more money. But this time it was with good news for a change: An arranger friend of his had a "friend of a friend" who could get me into the famed Bucks County Playhouse for the upcoming summer stock season and, hopefully, an apprenticeship which might finally earn me my Equity card.

And so, without thinking twice, I left California far behind—and the Pasadena Playhouse after only a year. Who knows what might have happened if I'd stayed there for the full two years?

Just look at what happened to Dustin Hoffman …

Summer Stock

I don't have to tell you how quickly I jumped at the chance to take my father up on his generous offer, and was on the bus to Pennsylvania before you could say "summer stock." For once having an inside track, I was suddenly a shoe-in and quickly hired on as what was known in those days as an "apprentice actor."

This was a fancy way of saying that, in addition to actually acting every once in awhile, I would also be required to set up the stage, break down the stage, build the sets, paint the sets, arrange the sets, and break them all down again before the next show began the following week. It was a roughneck life, what amounted to little more than the dressed up version of being a carnival worker—only with costumes and props instead of tattoos and cotton candy.

In return, they gave me room and board and, between what little money I could scrounge up on my own and what my father sent me each week to help out, I was able to eke out a living while learning my craft at what was then the premiere summer stock stage for budding actors of my generation.

The Bucks County Playhouse was then, and is now, a national landmark rich in theatrical history. Some of the biggest and brightest names in show business first got their start on its stage. The first show ever performed there was a drama, *Springtime for Henry*, starring the well known actor Edward Everett Horton who, as luck would have it, I would come to know quite well as the summer of 1956 passed. More on him later ...

The sparkling reputation of the Bucks County Playhouse grew rapidly after its inaugural season. It soon became known as America's Most Famous Summer Theatre, and for good reason. Not only did performances feature well-known stars of stage, screen and television, but the Playhouse also became known as a pre-Broadway theatre, premiering some of the most famous dramas in theatrical history. Dramas like *Harvey*, *Nobody Loves Me*, otherwise known as *Barefoot in the Park*, and *Give 'Em Hell Harry* all made their premieres at Bucks County.

The list of actors and actresses who have appeared at Bucks County Playhouse is impressive, to say the least. Kim Hunter, Helen Hayes, Colleen Dewhurst, Lillian Gish, June Lockhart, Frances Reid, Peggy McCay, Grace Kelly, Paul Lynde, Leslie Nielsen, Jack Klugman, Roddy McDowell, Walter

Matthau, Merv Griffin and Larry Hagman have all appeared in performances there.

Equal parts summer camp and Broadway "boot camp," being an apprentice actor at the Bucks County Playhouse was a dream come true for a twenty-year-old actor with stars in his eyes—and sawdust in his hair.

American University's Theater Department was great and I certainly learned an amazing amount at the Pasadena Playhouse, but Bucks County afforded me my first real taste of working with true stardom. Some were stars in their own mind, of course, but stars nonetheless.

It was a heady brew indeed …

With its close proximity to the fabled lights of Broadway, this former mill turned acting Mecca in Pennsylvania was at the time a tempting lure for many famous actors of its day to test their chops in new performances, revitalize their careers, or lick their wounds as the transition from radio to television left many former stars floundering as they struggled to keep up with so-called "modern technology."

Summer stock was the acting equivalent of a week-long Daytona 500 pit stop. Plays by some of the day's premiere playwrights were fine-tuned and smoothed out while the day's reining stars of stage and screen swooped in for a week or two of standing ovations and unbridled adulation as eager young apprentices like me watched spellbound from the wings.

Occasionally, we even got a chance to act …

Playing God

I knew I'd found my one true calling when my first onstage roll during that heady summer of 1956 was playing … *God.*

Literally …

Later to become a 1959 movie of the same name starring Zero Mostel and Charlotte Rae, the *The World of Sholom Aleichem* retold the stories of the great humorist who wrote *Fiddler on the Roof.* In one scene, I got the chance to play God.

Perhaps telling of my hubris during that summer, at the time I didn't even think it was much of a stretch!

But it wasn't the rolls that thrilled me that year, it was the co-stars. In *The World of Sholom Aleichem*, for instance, I shared the stage with a bonafide heavyweight of that era: Howard Da Silva.

A "local boy done good," Howard Da Silva had worked the steel mills of Pennsylvania to pay his way through Carnegie Institute. After finishing his acting training, Da Silva went to work for Eva Le Galliene's theatrical troupe. He brought attention to himself by staging a one-man show, *Ten Million Ghosts*, which led to several years' work with Orson Welles' Mercury Theatre.

On Broadway, the stocky, booming-voiced Da Silva created the roles of Jack Armstrong in *Abe Lincoln in Illinois* and Jud Frye in *Oklahoma*. When I wasn't trading lines with the Broadway legend, I loved to lean just offstage and listen to Da Silva orate. Like my other hero, Orson Welles, who could read the yellow pages and make you think they were Shakespeare, Da Silva had an equally commanding voice that made one sit up and take notice, even in scenes that would have been mundane in another actor's less capable hands.

In those days, microphones were still light years away. An actor's voice was all he had, and it had to project to the "cheap seats," way, way in the back next to the ashtrays and concession stand. Though it might have had "too much city in it" for the radio, my booming voice was nonetheless a treasured asset on the stage, and learning from stars like Howard Da Silva only made it just that much more so.

While I toiled away between my own live performances building sets and breaking them down, I soon got even more chances to co-star with some of the visiting luminaries who graced the Bucks County Playhouse stage that 1956 season.

Making her first appearance at the Playhouse that year, Billie Burke continued the season with *Solid Gold Cadillac* by Howard Teichmann and George S. Kaufman. "Solid gold" was an apt description for this undisputed legend, who was truly one of the great stars of all time. I'm sure you'll remember Ms. Burke from the 1939 film *The Wizard of Oz*, in which she played a role that must have come quite naturally to this good-natured grand dame: The good fairy.

Good witch, bad witch, devil or angel, I fell in love with Ms. Burke immediately. Though she urged us all to call her "Billie," not a one of us would. At the stately age of eighty-seven, she was just too big a star to call by her first name, even by the other Hollywood heavyweights who made their infrequent appearances that summer.

Ms. Burke was already getting old, and more than that—she could barely see! But the veteran actress didn't let anything as minor as near blindness stop her from pursuing her one true love. A gentle, loyal assistant would lead her on and off stage every performance, and the rest of us quickly learned to take up his slack as we silently maneuvered her around set with a well-placed nudge—or occasional forearm!

Though her eyes were weak, her delivery had never been stronger. Even approaching ninety, she knew the play inside and out. At least, that is, everybody *else's* part. Though she often had trouble reciting her own lines, it was far from a detriment. In fact, Ms. Burke's hilarious ad libs often made the play funnier than it really was.

As that summer's cavalcade of big-name stars and interesting roles forged ahead, Russell Nype starred with Jane Morgan in the drama, *Paris*.

Nype had already made a name for himself co-starring with Ethel Merman on Broadway in *Call Me Madam*, and co-star Jane Morgan was to star that very year in the successful adaptation of the popular TV series, *Our Miss Brooks*, starring Eve Arden as the wisecracking high school English teacher. You might also recall Miss Morgan's lovely singing voice on her million-seller hit, "Fascination."

I learned as much from both of these wonderful performers while trading lines with them onstage as I did watching them from the wings. I was like a vacuum cleaner, sucking everything in, listening, eavesdropping, always watching, watching. Every second, every minute.

And this was just the beginning for me …

I was also to share the stage that fateful season with another veteran actor named Jerome Cowan. Cowan was playing Justice Oliver Wendell Holmes in *The Magnificent Yankee*, a play based on Holmes' life written by Emmett Lavery. I was his personal secretary on stage that summer, and just as in *Detective Story*, even though the part was small, at least a few critics managed to notice me.

Please, Spell the Name Right

While starring in the 1935 Broadway hit *Boy Meets Girl*, Cowan was spotted by movie producer Sam Goldwyn, who cast Cowan as a sensitive Irish rebel in 1936's *Beloved Enemy*. Most of Cowan's subsequent films found him playing glib lawyers, shifty business executives, and jilted suitors.

When I first met him, Cowan was on a self-induced "leave of absence" from Hollywood, returning to his first love, the stage, and busily impressing greenhorn rookies like me and the rest of the "apprentice actors" with his air of sophistication and legendary stories of today's hottest stars.

Before long, Bucks County Playhouse wrapped up its summer stock theater for 1956 and, just like that, twelve weeks and eight shows went by faster than intermission at some Sunday matinee. At the beginning, I wondered how I would ever last the whole summer.

But now, with the end at hand, I realized I wanted twelve *more* weeks …

I knew I'd learned the ropes that eventful summer, and learned them from some of the very best, but likewise realized I had much, much more to learn before I could ever join their ranks. I said goodbye to friends both new and old, but secretly wished the summer didn't have to end.

Then again, I couldn't get my Equity card until it did …

A Match Made in … The Bronx?

1956 was a year full of lessons for me. My first was learning that getting your Equity card, and actually putting it to good use, were two very different things. I came home from Pennsylvania so full of myself I believe my parents needed a shovel just to dig me out. (My father also threatened to widen the front door to allow for my big head!) While my parents were naturally proud of their beaming son, I was obviously somewhat … prouder.

Like most young actors fresh off their first brush with success, I felt certain the roles would soon come calling, and that agents, producers, and directors would be knocking down my door at any minute. Once again, I had a lot to learn.

One such lesson was that there was no sure thing … as a *sure* thing.

Shortly after arriving back home in the Bronx a friend of a friend of a friend called from Miami, telling me about a play that I'd be "perfect for"

26

down in Florida. Once again, the timing couldn't have been more perfect. Summer was over and fall was upon us. With nothing to do anyway, and the weather getting colder, honing my craft in "the sunshine state" sounded like just the ticket. I immediately packed up and headed south to Coral Gables, Florida, home of the Coconut Grove Playhouse.

Once I'd arrived, however, I soon learned that someone else had already landed the role I was "just perfect for" and, suddenly, there I was, stranded in the hottest city on earth. Literally. As I sweated through several days of wondering where to go and what to do, I learned of a local theater that was one actor shy for their next big show. After auditioning, I finally landed a small part in *The 7 Year Itch* with Eddie Bracken, star of such lighthearted, escapist comedies and musicals as *Hold That Blonde* and *Ladies' Man*.

I wasn't in town long before I heard that a close friend, not to mention the guy who was dating my sister, Howie Maurer, was staying at a local hotel. A fantastic piano player, then as well as now, Howie later went on to fame and glory as a Vegas reverend, marrying hundreds of young newlyweds each year, despite the fact that he's as Jewish as they come!

Matchmaking must have been in Howie's blood, because not five seconds after showing up at his room old Howie got to work, handing me a stiff drink and more than the usual line of BS.

"Do I got a girl for you," said Howie with a wolfish grin. Having been on the receiving end of one too many of "Howie's girls," I groaned.

"Listen, Howie," I said, my eyes scanning the impromptu party happening in the other room, "before you tell me about a girl you found for me, who is that gorgeous thing dancing in the blue angora sweater?"

Howie followed my gaze, rolling his eyes as he said, *"That's* the girl I'm telling you about …"

And that was how I was introduced to the woman who would change, and eventually define, my very life: Toby Druger. A statuesque brunette with beautiful eyes, a gorgeous smile, and a petite, sexy body to match, I was instantly in lust with my feisty "blind date."

Even more so when I realized this was to be no long-distance relationship: Toby's family lived back in the Bronx, too! However, going from the East Bronx, where I lived, to see Toby in the West Bronx soon became quite a chore.

When I couldn't borrow my father's car, which was often the case as he was on the road traveling from orchestra pit to orchestra pit, I had to take both a train *and* a bus just to get to Toby's front door. But so what? I couldn't have cared less. She was sexy, beautiful, sweet, and really, really funny.

You'll find out just how funny later …

In addition to feeling I'd found someone really special with Toby, I immediately fell in love with her family as well. Her mother, Lillian Druger, was a secretary in the local public school system and, like most Jewish mothers, kept an immaculate home that was always overflowing with the inviting smells of fresh-cooked meals every time I walked in the house, morning, noon, or night.

Hal Druger, the patriarch of the family, was a spitfire of a little man standing scarcely taller than 5' 4" in stature, but miles high in integrity. His quiet, steady presence left an indelible impression on my life, then as now.

A milkman by trade, Hal used to get up at two a.m. and leave the house long before the rest of the family rose to drive his endlessly snaking route through the boroughs of the Bronx and back again, delivering the endlessly clanking bottles of milk that most surely would have driven a less content man quietly mad.

Though he was often preparing for bed just as I was swinging by to pick Toby up for one of our many weekly dates, Hal always found time to indulge in his favorite pastime: Writing—and reading—poetry. His thoughtful, engaging poetry was as quick to emit a laugh as it was a tear, and I spilled plenty of both as I grew to know, love, and respect Toby's dad.

Working his tail off as a milkman, he was there for Toby and her three siblings seven days a week, fifty-two weeks a year. So poor was the Druger family that the four children all had to share the same bedroom! I often said of Toby's family that "they were close because they *had* to be close." Hal was a sensitive and intelligent man, who I really cared deeply for.

But I felt closer still with his beautiful daughter.

Soon I would find out that she felt the same way, too ...

Theater Go-Round

As the summer of 1957 approached, Toby and I had plenty of time to court each other during all those sultry New York nights. Dinner and dancing (on the cheap, natch) soon took the place of acting and earning, as few new roles came my way during the first half of what would become a seminal year for me.

While I was still getting used to calling myself by the "stage name" I'd chosen to grace my brand new Equity card, "Jed Allan," the new *last* name was actually my old *middle* name and the spelling of Allan was to give me grief my entire career, I eventually got an audition for another popular acting venue at the time, Theater Go-Round in Virginia Beach, Virginia.

While the gig was for yet another popular summer stock season, the opportunity was much greater for me this "go round" than it had been back in Bucks County. While that venue had been a "star theater," so named for the big-name stars that were hustled in every other week to grace the stage before being whisked back to Broadway or Hollywood, Theater Go Round was what was known as a "resident theater."

This meant that there would be no set building and sawdust shuffling for old Jed Brown, ehhr, Allan, this time around. For once, I'd auditioned for and been hired as a "resident actor," which meant I'd be the one starring in the plays while others built the sets and broke them down.

It was a big step for me, and I intended to make the most of it ...

Of course, being a "resident actor" had its privileges. With no sets to build or sawdust to shuffle, I found myself with more time on my hands than usual. Taking advantage of it, Toby drove up with my cousin for a romantic, if brief, visit.

The pace in Virginia Beach was slower than that in the Bronx, with more room to move and less people to get in your way. Toby and I took long walks on the sand, dashing in and out of the ocean and sharing countless hours of unhurried conversation and smoldering glances.

Please, Spell the Name Right

It was to be an interlude, of sorts. With the heady rush of courtship shortly behind us and the pressures of love and marriage still in the distance, we were pleasantly sandwiched between the past and the future. There we lingered, sand in our feet, the salt spray on our lips as we kissed tenderly before Toby slid in next to my cousin for the long trip home.

Soon enough, it was right back to work …

Though I was to play in eight shows that season, I only really remember two of them: *Hat Full of Rain*, in which I played Polo, the part made famous to Tony Francioso in the movie of the same name, and "Bo" in the William Minsch play *Bus Stop* a part that Don Murray played in the movie adaptation.

As always, I learned quickly. I had to. There was no other way to star in eight plays a season without ramping up to speed in near record time. Rehearsals were short, directors' tempers were even shorter, and the only way to keep up was to stay alert. Lines had to be rehearsed, blocking laid out, and working with the same people week after week meant getting used to not only their personalities, but their peccadilloes too.

Little did I know it, but Bucks County had been a mere appetizer for the full eight course meal I was to swallow at Theater Go Round that summer. Some of the things I learned that season in Virginia surprised even me. I thought I'd seen big egos in Bucks County, but quickly learned that big egos evolved everywhere, regardless of the big accomplishments normally required to back them up.

The most important lesson of all was to be careful what you wish for. I'd dreamed of playing the starring roles so often and now, here I was, doing exactly that. But playing the starring role brought with it a host of pleasures—*and* complications.

It was a joy to do great plays written by great playwrights in front of enthusiastic and deserving audiences. But it was an awesome responsibility to be at the center of the whirlwind and carry it all off, night after night because now I was getting *paid* to. In live theater, you often work with up to a few hundred extras each night.

They're called "the audience."

Like the rest of us, sometimes they're up, other nights they're down. They can be tired, cranky, hungry, sore, old, young, loud, or worst of all, quiet. Lines that kill on Monday night fall dead on Tuesday, and vice versa.

A pratfall that had them rolling in the aisles one night leaves crickets chirping the next, and lines written by some of the country's finest playwrights can often sound as flat as week old beer if an audience is still chuckling over an untended "prop," as happened the night I looked down after several minutes of uncontrollable laughter to find my zipper wide open.

Holding an audience spellbound is a rush like no other. Hearing dead silence in a theater is an incredible feeling. (Unless you're doing a comedy, that is.) Otherwise, it means that you've got them in the palm of your hand and can take them anywhere you want to go.

Up, down, high, low, whatever the scene requires ...

They are there, in the moment, eating up every word, watching your every move, actually believing what you want them to believe, that you are the part you are playing that night: The philandering salesman or glib politician or doddering librarian or popular athlete. Above it all, you hear your voice booming all the way to the balconies.

When it was good, it was euphoric.

When it was bad, it was just plain painful.

Either way, I got some kind of an education that summer.

A summer I'll never forget.

How could I?

Before it was over, I was going to get married ...

An Indecent Proposal

Toby and I had been dating for nine long months when we decided on a quiet, moonlit drive into the city via the Washington Bridge one autumn night. It was well into 1957 by now, but the weather was still pretty enough for us to put the top down on my father's canary yellow Buick convertible.

With the Manhattan skyline shimmering as a backdrop, Toby cleared her throat and proposed to me as only a single Jewish girl from the Bronx could: "Jed, I think it's time you either shit or get off the pot!" (Well, she didn't really say it *that* way.)

"Excuse me," I deadpanned, knowing where this conversation was going but desperate to stall for time. Already I could feel my hands growing clammy around my father's oversized steering wheel.

"Are you ever going to marry me or what?" she asked petulantly, her gorgeous eyes blinking in the crisp fall breeze even as her full, red lips pursed with declaration.

"Jesus," I groaned. "But things are going so good for us. Why do you wanna go and mess it up by getting married?"

Her silence told me this was the wrong approach. Biting the bullet, I took another tact: "All right, all right, but can I have twenty-four hours to think it over?"

"You gotta be kidding me," she snapped, rolling her eyes and not letting me off the hook as easily as I'd hoped. "I can't believe you. Listen, you've got twenty-four hours, but if you still don't want to get married by tomor-row, this is our last date. I'm nineteen years old and I want to have kids while I'm young …"

"You just may have uttered one sentence too many," I thought to my-self as the sweat really started to pour off my face. But I just couldn't let her go and so, after a sleepless night spent tossing and turning, the next day I picked Toby up as usual—and proposed.

Well, sort of.

"Okay, okay," I sighed as soon as we were in the car. "We'll get married. Happy?"

"Don't do me any favors," she snorted by way of acceptance, pulling away.

I grabbed her and kissed her and told her that I loved her. And that was the brightest move I've ever made.

Then again, not giving her a ring at the time was not quite as bright a move …

Still, Toby and I chose to call this glaring omission "frugal." I was a starving actor; she was a starving college student studying to be a teacher.

Where was I gonna get the money for a ring when, after all, it was like pulling teeth just to get me to propose in the first place?

Others, however, might call it "cheap."

Toby's little brother, for one. A wiseass thirteen-year-old while I was proposing to his nineteen-year-old sister, George Druger (now "Dr. George Druger," a leading pulmonary specialist in Honolulu, Hawaii) was clearly ready for his bar mitzvah.

Now, I barely had enough for movie money, this in a time when a local matinee cost just twenty-five cents, let alone money to buy his sister an engagement ring, but I knew I had to give the kid something for this sacred Jewish coming of age ritual. A ritual I had gone through myself. So I reached down, dug deep, and did the best I could. To this day, Dr. George Druger calls my five bucks "the cheapest gift he's ever received."

But I take offense. Those five 1957 dollars would be worth at least … *ten* … today!

Sure … try a hundred.

Show Stopping at the "Show Shop"

For the third summer in a row, I was invited back to take the stage at summer stock. Completing my triumvirate of popular theaters, the summer of 1958 found me working at the long since forgotten Canton "Show Shop" just outside of Hartford, Connecticut.

Unlike the Theater Go-Round, which was a resident theater, the Show Shop was another star company. As actors, set directors, producers, and directors descended on the quiet town from both Hollywood and New York, I soon realized that many of the same players I'd met at Bucks County Playhouse were reuniting in Connecticut. Like a circuit, they seemed to travel from one popular playhouse to the next, forming small alliances and close cliques that, I suddenly realized, now included … *me*.

It was a different Jed Allan who got off a Greyhound bus in 1958 as summer filled Connecticut with lush green grasses and a population ready for eight long weeks of live theater featuring some of the biggest names in the biz. Equity card in hand, plenty of star names to drop at the ready, and two summers full of experience under my belt, I was ready to take the stage as the Show Shop's "resident juvenile."

Much like a designated batter, it was my job to assume all of the younger male rolls in productions that season. While legitimate stars were flown in from both coasts to fill the male and female lead roles, the rest of us "hired hands" found ourselves quickly typecast as "resident this" or "resident that."

From the older actors who played every grandma and spinster to the twenty-something actors like myself who found themselves playing everything from high school sports heroes to blushing newlyweds, we wore as many hats as we did corsets, helmets, sandals, and tuxedoes that magical season.

Some reunions were pleasant, others not so much. I immediately spotted Russell Nype, with whom I'd worked in the play *Paris* back at Bucks County two years earlier. Nype, who was later to star in *Love Story* with Steve McQueen and Ali McGraw, soon grew miffed because I was getting better reviews as the "resident juvenile" when we starred together in *Under the Yum-Yum Tree.*

The reviews came out on Friday, and by Saturday Nype had suddenly decided that, as he put it, he was "better for my role." (Though the critics begged to differ.) Now, we only played each show for a total of eight performances each week, and a new show was set to start the following Friday.

With Mondays being "dark," or the theater term for our much-needed day off, this meant that only four performances remained. But even better, he wanted me to learn his part by the following Tuesday! Three days of extra work for a total of three performances played, all so the "star" of the show could shine all the brighter.

Naturally, I refused …

It was a valuable, but timely, lesson to learn: Never upstage "the star," no matter how big a baby he might be. I worked with lots of stars that year, and many were kind, gracious, lovable human beings. Others not so much. Each of them, I discovered, had two sides: The public and the private.

Just like I had at Bucks County, I performed in several plays at the

Canton Show Shop that season, among them *Sweet Bird of Youth*. In the celebrated play by Tennessee Williams, actress-singer Edie Adams played Alexandra Del Lago while I played Chance Wayne, the part Paul Newman played on Broadway and later played in the 1962 film version.

Needless to say, I enjoyed acting opposite the beautiful blonde who I'd admired for years on the TV's *The Ernie Kovacs Show*, and who had recently won a Tony for her work in *Lil Abner*. It was stars like Edie who made these summers so memorable, but sometimes even the stars' spouses could leave our tongues wagging long after the summer was through.

Case in point, Ernie Kovacs himself, who came to our humble Show Shop to watch his wife Edie in *Sweet Bird of Youth*. He stayed the entire week during which the show ran and I have to tell you that I was in awe of him from the moment I met this larger than life entertainer. What a talent he was; truly a performing innovator. Getting to know Ernie during that week was one of the great moments in my life at the time.

And, as I think about it, even now ...

Tragically, only a few weeks after I met him, this sweet, kind, gentle man died prematurely in an automobile accident when, unbelted, he fell out of the driver's side door of his car and cracked his head on the unforgiving sidewalk. His passing was mourned by the world, and one struggling actor in particular, not just for his talent but the truly great guy that he was.

One of the last shows I did that season was *Black Sheep of the Family*. In *Black Sheep*, I got to work with another Hollywood legend, Edward "Everett" Horton, who played the role of the father in that play.

Horton was much more than just a fellow actor to me; he was one of the funniest men I'd ever met. While many actors and actresses viewed live theater much like a Hollywood movie set, repeating their lines the same way, with the same inflection, at the same time, over and over again, night after night, it was the rare dramatist like Horton who put the "live" back in live theater.

So comfortable in his role was he that Horton would inevitably talk and talk and talk, liberally ad libbing to the already meaty roll of the father in the play we shared. It was great for the audience, who night after night got more than their money's worth as they roared at Horton's blistering improvisations, and a hoot for those backstage, but for the actors on stage with Horton who were waiting for some kind of cue as to when we should give our measly little lines, it could frequently be a pain in the ass.

But as I got to know him, I soon grew over this stumbling block. As one of his rip-roaring soliloquies eventually wound down, Horton would silently nod at me, giving me the signal that it was—finally—my turn to speak. Once I grew comfortable with "the Horton method," as I eventually came to call it, I too could enjoy Horton's magical ad libs along with the audience.

In later years, Horton would form an equally valuable bond with a friend of mine, Joe Ross. When Horton fell ill toward the latter years of his life, Joe actually became his caretaker. This was something that came naturally to the sensitive and caring Ross, who's taken care of me more times over the years than I care to remember!

After his passing, Joe was thrilled—and horrified—to learn that Horton had left him a case of vintage wine worth over $2,500. Touched, because a man like Horton would remember him with such a grand gesture. Horrified, because the bottles were so valuable he was afraid to open any of them!

He'd tried once, popping the cork and savoring an acrid aroma that was foul enough to intimidate him into thinking priceless, vintage wine was supposed to smell like rotting sulfur. One taste, however, told him his sense of smell was right on the money: As will occasionally happen, the bottle had gone bad after so many years probably due to a decayed cork.

Ross was horrified, not only because he wouldn't be able to enjoy any of the rest of the bottles, but also because he knew Horton would be upset that his parting gesture could never be truly appreciated. Ribbing him, I urged Joe not to be so chicken and give another bottle a try. He did, and found the taste superb. Apparently, the only bad bottle in the case had been the first one opened.

Travelers to Encino, California may recognize Horton's name, if not for his impressive filmography than at least for his close proximity. After all, his name graces the Edward "Everett" Horton bridge that passes over the popular 101 freeway.

Jed Allan

It is a fitting tribute to a great man …

Another legend who already had my admiration, but soon won my friendship, that summer was a veteran actor and bonafide war hero named Wayne Morris. A fellow alum, Morris had been discovered at the acclaimed Pasadena Playhouse by a talent scout for Warner Brothers.

Since then, the larger than life actor had starred on stage and screen. I'd watched him for years playing tough guy roles and to see him up close and personal made him seem twice as big. Perhaps, that's because he was.

Though we both stood about 6' 3" tall, at 240-pounds he outweighed me by a good eighty pounds. Tough as nails and salt of the earth, Morris and I instantly hit it off and shared many a late night cruising up and down the streets of Bucks County, PA, which really only had two things to offer us: Bars and antique shops.

It wasn't much of a choice and, over cold beer and stale peanuts, Morris and I traded war stories about "the biz," with me running out long before happy hour and leaving Morris to tell the lion's share as he regaled me well into the wee hours. At least three or four of the ten days I had to carry that massive S.O.B. home on my own wobbly legs, but it never seemed to deter him. The man never missed a curtain call the entire season.

Then again, he never missed "last call" either …

Like Ernie Kovacs before him, however, Morris died too young. He suffered a massive heart attack while visiting an aircraft carrier in San Francisco Bay and was pronounced dead after being transported to the Naval Hospital in Oakland, California. He was only forty-five, and left behind too many heartbroken Americans who loved and admired the man. Arguably, his biggest fan was a scrawny kid from the Bronx who was more grateful for the brief friendship he'd shared with the gruff, burly star than for his long string of popular movies.

Special Delivery

I got quite a surprise as that summer season in Canton wound down and stages, sets, and friendships were slowly being packed away for another long year. Instead of boarding yet another crowded Greyhound bus for the inevitably meandering trip back to the Bronx, I got a "special delivery" of sorts when a five-year-old Chrysler rolled up to my rented room carrying two of my favorite passengers: My fiancée and my father!

Without me knowing anything about it, they had gone together to purchase the car as what amounted to an early wedding present for me. I was both thrilled, and terrified, at the same time. For one, it was the most thoughtful gesture I believe anyone had ever made on my behalf. Despite being a few years old, the car was a beauty and would give me the freedom to go on as many auditions as I could, and not be hampered by bus, train, or taxi schedules.

On the other hand, a premature wedding gift given to me by my future bride and my grinning (one might say shit-eating-grinning) father was tantamount to securing the ball and chain straight to my leg.

My first thought as I saw them standing against that car was, "Oh wow!"

My second thought was, "Oh *shit!*"

That was it. My life was over. No doubt Toby's name was on the registration, and in one fell swoop she had managed to weasel her way into both my heart—*and* my driveway. Now there was no escaping the sanctity of marriage. Tossing my bags into the large trunk, these three amigos headed back to New York with one nervous groom-to-be at the wheel.

Amazingly enough, it wasn't the only surprise I got that year ...

Several weeks after Dad, Toby and I drove home from Canton, with few acting leads on my dance card and a wedding date looming over my head like a doomed man finally spies the gallows, I made a suggestion of my own to my good friend Artie Lauer: "Let's join the army."

Far from being patriotic, the decision was much more about being another "p" word: Practical. I was literally petrified of getting married and, in those days, joining up for the Army reserves meant little more than a six month commitment—and a steady paycheck.

At the time, both seemed equally appealing ...

Struggling as an actor and weighed down by the pressures of an impending marriage, albeit to the woman of my dreams, I rashly decided to chuck both and take a half-year hiatus, courtesy of Uncle Sam.

Going down to the nearest recruiter's office, I soon found myself looking forward to the promise of "three hots and a cot," not to mention extending my engagement for an extra six months and, quite possibly, a lifetime.

Artie wasn't quite as enthusiastic about the idea, but he'd do anything for a friend and, after all, it seemed like a good idea at the time. In front of God and country, Artie and I eagerly signed our letters of intent, and then proceeded to be given a thorough physical by a local doctor.

Artie, who was more concerned with helping his old buddy out of a jam than he was actually serving Uncle Sam for the next six months, passed his exam with flying colors. As for myself, my rheumatic fever as a child, which kept me in bed for seven months when I was eleven-years-old, left me undesirable to the Army.

So while Artie headed off to basic training, determined, I'm sure, never to do a "good buddy" another favor again, I was 4-F!

Both of us, it seemed, were getting "hitched."

For better or worse.

So much for an extended engagement …

At the Chupa!

After being turned down by the army, I resigned myself to another form of basic training: Being engaged. Toby and I were kicking around wedding dates one day shortly after we all returned from my summer at the Canton Show Shop, when my father made a helpful—if unwelcome—suggestion.

"Didn't you just get that ten-day gig at the Mercury Edsel Lincoln show out in California?" he asked, apropos of nothing, referring to my latest acting job, an industrial show for a brand new car being introduced by the famous automobile manufacturer.

"Sure," I shrugged, wondering where this was heading and confident that the punch line, as usual, *wouldn't* be in my favor. "It's in less than a month."

"So," pop had casually suggested, whipping Toby into a frenzy as she listened intently, "you'll be away for ten days, they're footing the bill, what do they care if one more person tags along? You can call it a 'working honeymoon.' It's the perfect solution."

"But the show's in three weeks," I countered, hoping to prolong the inevitable for up to three years, if at all possible. "Surely we can't put on a wedding in three … *short* … weeks." (Sometimes it really *does* help to be an actor.)

Not surprisingly, this was not the kind of negative thinking an overeager Jewish fiancée was going to take sitting down. Toby took it as a personal challenge and, to her credit, pulled off the impossible. In twenty-one short days, she managed to book a room, invite friends, order a cake, brush up on the inevitable Jewish wedding traditions, and even hire a rabbi.

Well, sort of …

It was what I would call a "semi-traditional" Jewish wedding attended by about fifty to sixty people, mostly family and a few close friends, and presided over by the only man that Toby could find who was legally qualified to marry us with such little notice: A non-denominational Jewish "rabbi" reverend. If that sounds silly, it probably was, because he didn't have the title "rabbi." (For the sake of my forty-three years of marriage, I hope it was legal.)

The only thing "traditional" about the wedding ceremony was that it took place under a *chupah*, the instantly recognizable canopy that has long been recognized as a symbol of the home to be built and shared by the couple.

The chupah is usually held outside, under the stars, as a sign of the blessing given by God to Abraham that his children shall be "as the stars of the heavens." In our case, however, our painted plywood chupah was smack in the middle of a rented social hall decked out by the indomitable Toby to look as close to a synagogue as possible, Rabbi-Reverend Jared Newman presiding.

I knew we were in trouble when, as Rabbi-Reverend Newman bent over in prayer during one of the *many* blessings we endured that day, and, for the life of me, I swear I spied that afternoon's racing form poking out from beneath the good book!

Under the chupah, a glass was finally placed on the floor, and I eagerly shattered it with my size-twelves. Traditionally, this act is supposed to symbolize the last time the groom gets to "put his foot down." But try telling *that* to the new Mrs. Jed Allan Brown, aka Janice Toby Allan Brown aka Toby Allan Brown aka Toby …

Mr. and Mrs. Edsel

My wedding night with Toby was memorable to say the least, but not in the way you might think. Around midnight, as Toby and I lounged in our decidedly *non*-honeymoon suite at the Grand Concourse Hotel in the Bronx, we received a surprisingly firm knock at our door.

Toby was surprised when she answered it to find one of my friends leaning on the door in a drunken stupor. But she was even more surprised when, from out in the hall, five more of my drunken friends rushed past her—once they'd determined she was dressed and they weren't "interrupting" anything, that is—and picked me up.

They then decided to hoist me on their arms and carry me around the hotel lobby like a conquering hero for close to an hour, depositing me back in my room just after one a.m. to a miffed but slightly bemused Mrs. Toby Allan. I might not have minded so much if it wasn't the first night of my honeymoon.

Or if I didn't have to get up at seven the next morning to catch my flight to California …

I can still recall the theme song I performed at the Mercury Edsen Lincoln Show in November of 1958:

"Mercury Shows You What New Really Means

Mercury Shows You What New Really Means

See Mercury and Then You'll See What New Really Means …"

Not exactly "Sunrise, Sunset," but what do you expect from the same folks who brought you the Edsel? In those days, car shows were one of the few chances a working actor had of making great money in a short amount of time. It was also a chance for me to show off some of what I'd learned in my year back at the Pasadena Playhouse. Back then, such industrial shows consisted of singing, dancing, and, not surprisingly, driving! (Personally, I would have rather fenced, but hey—a buck's a buck.)

But it's not all fun and games. Dressed to the nines, I got an honorary degree in stock car driving from shows such as this first one, and subsequent appearances at similar shows for Buick, Lincoln, Chevy, and even … Campbell's Soup.

Performers were almost exclusively male, as they had to perform elaborate stunts such as driving up and down steep ramps to the gasps of an adoring crowd, or perhaps even performing risky parallel parking maneuvers—hazardous in the best of situations, especially in the Bronx—on a revolving stage. A native New Yorker, fortunately I had this angle covered.

Other driving disasters were narrowly diverted. I once had to drive a new car from inside the trunk! Angling a mirror just so, I learned to maneuver a custom-designed steering wheel and gas pedal from behind the back seat, unseen, so it looked like the car actually "drove itself." This would have been a challenge for an actor standing 5' 3", but try cramming an extra foot of me in there!

Still, it was a great way to make $250 for a week's worth of work, nice money in those days, and just as nice a place to spend your honeymoon. Toby and I enjoyed our ten days in California, soaking up the sunshine in between dance routines, parallel parking, and catchy jingles that, despite being corny, still left my angora-sweater wife swooning in the aisles.

As for myself, I was enjoying both of my favorite pastimes at once: Being with Toby and working as an actor. I'd put in my time in summer stock theater, working on my chops at Bucks County Playhouse, Canton's Show Stop, and Theater Go-Round, and now I was singing and dancing my way through sunny California on behalf of the country's newest automobile.

Too bad the car wasn't as successful as the show! Tanned, rested, and more importantly, *married*, Toby and I returned to New York as man and wife, determined to make both our marriage—and our careers—a success.

Little did we know how long both might last …

Going Bonkers in Yonkers

Our first home together was a basement apartment in the heart of Yonkers. Barely in our twenties and quickly losing our healthy California tans, we rented the lower half of a house occupied by the most unattractive middle-aged couple I'd ever met in my entire life. (And that's saying a lot for someone from the Bronx.)

They were kind people, though, with hearts as big as the pores on their broad, coarse faces, and our rent was more than likely the cheapest in town. For the privilege, we were constantly invited to the couple's grape pressing parties, as they often reveled in making homemade wine in the cellar.

We graciously turned them down each time, as much for the dress code as for the festivities: Born nudists, our bulbous landlords preferred to crush their grapes in the buff, lavishing in the juicy pleasures of their dual passions: Nudity and homemade wine.

Instead, Toby and I not-so-gratefully accepted the fruits of their labors: Too sweet wine in old beer bottles that we made a great show of appreciating before secretly disposing of every time we left the house!

Toby put her degree in education to good use as a first through fourth grade teacher at a local elementary school. Then, as now, kids were tough and none was tougher than the daughter of boxing legend himself, Floyd Patterson, one of Toby's first students that year.

Watching Toby come home tired and distraught each day after school sent my protective instincts into overdrive. Quietly, I taught her all the pressure points of a human body, schooling the first year teacher in how to stop a rampaging child in his tracks—without leaving any telltale marks on their roughneck little bodies.

It was a skill that had come in handy growing up on the tough streets of the Bronx, but one that came in even handier in the even rougher classrooms of Yonkers …

Statute of Limitations

As for myself? While Toby waged war in the world of formal education I took odd jobs around town in between auditioning for any kind of acting work I could find. My favorite was at a famous haberdashery that, for legal reasons both real and imagined, shall remain anonymous.

There I toiled in the "will call" office, where the lords and ladies of high

Please, Spell the Name Right

New York fashion came to pick up their mink stoles and tailored suits before dashing off to yet another downtown ball or charity event.

They say you can take the boy out of the Bronx, but just try taking the Bronx out of the boy. I'm here to say that I'm living proof! As my fledgling acting career stalled in the wake of "love and marriage," I continued to go on auditions in suits as scruffy as I was.

Despite my painfully thin wallet, I'd always managed to be a dapper dresser. I didn't like not looking sharp, ever, and so I decided I needed a better wardrobe to wear to auditions. With little money and less prospects, I pulled the old bait and switch that I'm hoping fans both young and old will forgive of a starving artist—not to mention a hungry young husband.

Once a month, for about three months, I would pick a suit off the racks that caught my eye. Pinstripes. Gray flannel. Didn't matter, as long as it was in my size and would impress a casting director. Boxing it up in the "will call" office, I would then forge a ticket in the name of "Harry A. Smith" and wait until said customer walked in to pick up "his" suit. Handing it over gladly, I jovially wished "Mr. Smith" good day and went about my business.

Later that day, clocked out and paranoid, I would stroll into Grand Central Station to board the long train ride home to our basement apartment under the nudist winemakers in Yonkers. With one slight detour: Dropping a nickel into a pay locker, I would pick up Mr. Smith's suit and, in return, leave him five bucks for his trouble before sealing the locker shut.

Naturally, I took them elsewhere to be tailored …

Taxi Cab Confessions

I worked at said haberdashery for a mere three months, liberating no more than one suit per month from its overflowing inventory. But despite my short tenure there, these three suits were to last me for the next five years. (Too bad I can't name the store, that sounds like quite the endorsement!)

Once I had a full closet, I quickly left the scene of the crime—and hopefully my criminal past—far, far behind and began driving a checkered cab around the crowded streets of Manhattan. The pay was slightly better—on a good night I could bring home twenty-five dollars—and I thought it would be a welcome respite from the stuffy atmosphere of a department store.

Jed Allan

I was wrong …

Driving a checkered cab around the city five days a week was about as far from the stage as I could possibly get. Except, that is, when I picked up passengers after a Sunday matinee on Broadway.

Rarely did I go home without a migraine headache from the constant stop and start of big city driving, or a sore neck from straining to see if a potential passenger was waving me down, or simply waving to a friend across the street.

I did a fair amount of driving in rough parts of the city, and had to be careful about who I picked up when darkness inevitably fell. A man alone was a sure bet. I figured I could take just about anyone one on one if I had to. A man and a woman? Sure. Okay. But I never picked up two men at the same time.

Then again, not all customers were quite what they seemed. One night I picked up a verbose fellow clutching a paper sack as if it held the family jewels. Pulling up to the curb, he quickly stumbled into the backseat before I could size him up properly.

"Take me to 27th and Broadway," he ordered as I pulled from the curb into heavy afternoon traffic.

"Sure thing," I offered, hoping to start off on the right foot.

"Hey," he soon bellowed, "you're taking me the wrong way."

Soon, the insults flooded from the backseat: "I'm no sucker. You're ripping me off. We're going in circles. See if you get a tip from me!"

Unable to stand it any longer, I replied, "Don't tip me, pal, I could give a damn. Just shut the hell up or I'll call a cop."

Still the insults and epithets poured from the backseat. Finally, I could take it no more and, as soon as I spotted a beat cop on the side of the road, I immediately pulled over and caught his attention.

"Listen, officer," I said, explaining my situation as best I could, "I've got this passenger and he's giving me nothing but verbal abuse. Can you do something about it?"

"There's nothing I can do for you, pal," pleaded the cop. "But the precinct is right around the corner. Pull around and drop him off, someone there can help you."

Please, Spell the Name Right

We never made it that far. Knowing the mouthy gent would never stand still for being hauled into a precinct by a lowly cab driver, our exchanges grew hotter and heavier until I pulled the car over, jerked the cab to a halt, and opened his door for him. One last insult was all I needed when the patronizing passenger lurched out of the car, looking for all the world as if he was ready to throw a roundhouse punch.

Thinking a fistfight was inevitable, I clocked him one on the side of the head as he was getting out of the car. "Always get in the first punch" was my motto when driving a cab. But much to my surprise, the man with such a big mouth barely came up to my chest. Feeling horrible, I leaned down to help him up from the pavement. But instead of accepting my silent apology, he blinked his bleary eyes—and opened his mouth.

"Is that all you got?" he shrieked from his perch in the gutter, where he lay there holding onto his paper bag, which I could now see was full of liquor bottles, most of them half empty. "I just took your best shot. Is that all you got? Is that all you got?!?"

I left him lying by the side of the road, screaming into the rearview mirror, "I took your best shot. Is that all you got?"

For all I know, he's still lying there today …

(Straight Out of) Central Casting

In 1959 I got my first agent.

Well, sort of …

Toby was still teaching the tough kids in Yonkers and I was still driving my cab in the city, often dressed to the nines in my purloined pinstripes as I had to schedule my auditions in between pick-ups and drop-offs.

Headaches, backaches, and strained necks still plagued me, and as tough as she had it herself, Toby took pity on her working stiff husband and begged a family friend of hers named Bernie Styles to get me acting gigs from time to time.

Bernie owned a New York agency called Central Casting, and was able to give me several big breaks that first year we worked together. Though we never signed a formal contract, I was unofficially a client and he came through like a trooper every time Toby called him with an impassioned plea on my behalf.

It would be years before Bernie finally told me of Toby's frantic phone calls to his office that year, and I'm sure I would have put a stop to them if I'd known about them at the time, but I've always been eternally grateful for the gigs, the experience, the credits, and especially the much-needed money they provided a starving young married couple living with nudists in the Yonkers wine country.

Rarely were the opportunities anything a veteran actor might call "significant," but they were nothing short of solid gold to a man in my position. Mostly they were "under fives," the industry term for being "an extra with fewer than five lines." But through them I was able to add such 1950s classic films as *Mirage* and *Andy*, among dozens of others, to my rapidly growing resume.

I was soon to learn that, despite all the help he'd given me, not to mention the fact that he ran one of the most successful talent agencies in New York, Bernie was not exactly a big fan of actors. In fact, beside myself, the only other actor he favored was another talented "under fiver" named Frank Wayne, aka Frank Weinberger.

And though he wasn't the biggest fan of his growing stable of successful actors, loyalty was one of the man's strong suits. Throughout the years, Frank and I still received regular phone calls from this amazingly talented—and loyal—agent, aka friend who, by the way, is still going strong at eighty-five. As a matter of fact, Bernie is currently my neighbor, living less than two miles from me in Southern California. We're still good friends to this day.

Maybe even more so …

Blue Skies, Smiling at Me

As the innocent 50s drew to a close and the turbulent 60s loomed uncertainly on the horizon of a country whose peace was slow to shatter, I was asked once again to return to Bucks County Playhouse in 1959.

That final season of the 1950s opened with *The Tunnel of Love* by Joseph

Fields and Peter DeVries and starred Rita Gam, Scott McKay, Sono Osato and Jack Pyle. *Summer of the 17th Doll* followed *The Tunnel of Love* and starred James Whitmore.

Short and stocky, with a gruff, weather-beaten face and wry smile, James Whitmore earned his first Oscar nomination for his supporting role in 1949's *Battleground*, only his second film. Despite the critical nod, Whitmore had found it rough going in the beginning of his career, mainly because of his startling resemblance to none other than Spencer Tracey.

The play we were in together that final summer of the 50s revolved around a town and concerned itself with the eventual realization that the two central characters aren't as young as they used to be. Opposite James Whitmore was another 50s legend, Art Lund.

Once again, working on *Summer of the 17th Doll* afforded me an opportunity to work with someone I'd known and admired for years. Blessed with a beautiful voice and a storied career, Art Lund had a hit record with Benny Goodman's orchestra back in 1946 called "Blue Skies," by Irving Berlin:

Blue skies smilin' at me
Nothin' but blue skies do I see
Bluebirds singin' a song
Nothin' but bluebirds all day long

But Lund's talents went far beyond hit records with the country's most popular swing band. Though I must confess, it was his music that first brought us together. As a musician in many of Broadway's most popular and storied "pits," my father often brought me along with him to watch a Sunday matinee or two.

One of my favorites had been *The Most Happy Fella*, a lavish musical with music and lyrics by none other than Frank Loesser, who also wrote *Guys & Dolls* and, not surprisingly, starring his wife Lynn Loesser.

Adapted from Sidney Howard's 1924 play, *They Knew What They Wanted*, Frank Loesser's *The Most Happy Fella* revolved around the complications that arise when Tony, an aging Italian vineyard owner proposes by mail to Rosabella, a young waitress who once served him in a San Francisco restaurant. Rosabella has no recollection of Tony, but accepts his proposal largely because he has sent her a picture of Joe, his handsome ranch hand.

The Most Happy Fella opened at the Imperial Theatre on May 3, 1956 with a cast that featured Robert Weede as Tony, Jo Sullivan as Rosabella, and Art Lund as Joe. The show enjoyed a run of 676 performances.

One of the songs from the play, sung by none other than Art Lund himself, was called "Joey." I fell in love with the song, and admired Art's work so much, that I forced my musician father to drag me into the city with him every time he could. By the time the show had run its course, I'd seen Art Lund sing "Joey" no less than twenty-five times.

Now I was sharing a stage with him …

A Tiger at the Gates …

The second offering of 1959 was a play called *Tiger at the Gates* starring Hurd Hatfield, Philip Bourneuf, and Frances Reid. It was the first time that the play was produced professionally in the region and in the supporting cast was a young actor named … well, you'll find out shortly.

Set in and around the Palace of Troy, *Tiger at the Gates* was a drama written by Jean Giraudoux. Giraudoux's play, originally bearing the ironic title *The Trojan War Will Not Take Place*, was an allegory and a satire directed chiefly at man's propensity for making war.

Playing the lead role of Aristophanes, Hurd Hatfield was an American leading man best known for his portrayal of the title character in the Oscar-winning 1945 film *The Picture of Dorian Gray*.

A native of New York, Hatfield came to England to study acting at the Chekhov Theatre Studio in Devonshire. Despite numerous roles in scores of other movies, television and stage productions, he was forever associated with his staring role in the film version of the Oscar Wilde novel. He later became a lifelong friend of Angela Lansbury when they were making *Dorian Gray* together, and he guested twice on her successful TV series *Murder, She Wrote*.

In the role of Hecuba was none other than Frances Reid. Born in Wichita Falls, Texas, Frances was raised in Berkeley, California, where she was a fellow alum at The Pasadena Community Playhouse.

Please, Spell the Name Right

Her first radio job was at NBC as Ann Rutledge in *Prologue to Glory*, while her television credits include *The Eleventh Hour, Little Mister, Wagon Train,* and the movie-of-the-week, *Mercy or Murder?*

Though we first met in *Tiger at the Gates* that year, our friendship was to be rekindled years later in a very different venue: Frances Reid is the Emmy Award nominee who has played Alice Horton for the entire thirty-seven years that *Days of Our Lives* has been on the air. As one of the two remaining original cast members, she is indisputably one of the most revered veterans in soap opera history.

Best known for her Oscar-winning role as Nurse Rached in the film *One Flew over the Cuckoo's Nest,* Louise Fletcher played Helen of Troy that year. As for myself? I played yet another supporting role that came just a little too easily: Ajax, the drunken general of the guards. But more notable than my performance that year was the friendship I gained with another promising young actor who rounded out our cast playing Paris, the young male lead: Robert Redford.

Redford and I ate breakfast together every morning that summer, two young up and comers who found kinship over bacon and eggs in our favorite of Bucks County's artsy eateries.

We were all impressed by Redford's inherent brilliance, easy charm, and a face that wasn't exactly chopped liver. He was as cordial offstage as on, and I enjoyed watching him work, never dreaming how big a star he might become.

Another summer of stars both fading and emerging ended as the fall of 1959 crept on leaden feet into Pennsylvania's Bucks County. With the last set struck and our paychecks issued, Redford, the rest of the cast, and I went our separate ways.

For a while, anyway …

… And a Friend on the Street

Later that year, I ran into Bob on a cold windy street in mid-town Manhattan. It had only been a few months since we'd worked together and, even then, he wasn't a guy you forgot too quickly.

Slowing to greet him, I tapped him on the shoulder and, instead of the big smile of recognition I was expecting, he looked at me with saddened eyes and greeted me perfunctorily as we shared a quick hug on the streets.

Bob didn't look too good that day. In fact, he looked pretty bad. His face seemed somehow weathered, as if he'd gone through a hard, fast storm. Shuffling his feet, he greeted me by name before lapsing into an awkward silence.

"Are you keeping busy?" I asked, if only for something to say. It was a common greeting among actors, the thespian version of "How's it hanging?"

"They're closing the show," he mumbled, his strong voice trailing off in the winter chill. Bob was then playing in *The Hanging Tree*, a play based on the novel by Dorothy M. Johnson which details the character study of a doctor who saves a local criminal from a mob who is trying to hang him, but then tries to control the life of the young man, realizing that he can exploit his secret. I could tell the closing of the show had affected him, but we'd all been there and, frankly, I sensed there was more behind his shuffling feet and downcast eyes.

"Is something wrong, Bob? You wanna talk?" I asked him, sensing that something was not right.

"Actually, yeah," he said to me. "Besides the closing of the show, what happened is something that seems like a nightmare. I'm trying to get through it, so is my wife." He turned away, barely able to speak.

"My baby son died. I'm sorry," he went on, "I can't talk anymore." Then he turned around and walked away.

There was nothing I could say to make it better, nor would there ever be and, unfortunately, our paths have not crossed since.

The 60s:

From Live Theater to Live Television—An Actor's Journey

The 50s were finally over and I began the 60s as a young man wearing many hats: A professional actor, a married man, a working stiff. I had done my time in Summer Stock, earned my SAG card, and was officially a resident of the acting community in none other than New York City itself.

Like the song says, "If I can make it there …"

Well, I hadn't quite made it yet, but I was sure as hell trying.

Toby and I were slowly rounding the corner on our first wedding anniversary and had managed to leave the nudist winemakers behind in Yonkers, settling instead into our new digs in Rego Park, Queens. It was a family neighborhood, figuratively and literally speaking.

My aunt and uncle lived just up the street, and my sister Sandy lived with her new husband Johnny Parker a few blocks away. Johnny was a trumpet player of some note who had gigged with, among others, Thelonious Monk.

Probably one of the strangest men I'd ever met, he seemed to live in a world unto his own. But he needed a lot of different worlds, because after he and my sister broke up, Parker would go on to get married eight more times. He was successful, though, I'll give him that, writing many theme songs for many television shows.

But their divorce was still several years away and, for now, they were merely our happily married neighbors. Meanwhile, Mr. and Mrs. Jed Allan toiled away like so many other native New Yorkers just trying to make a living that turbulent decade. Toby was still teaching and I was still driving a cab, but not for long.

The 1960s brought with them more than space flight, Vietnam, and the Beatles. For me, it would be a year of crushing lows that brought about self-doubt and frustration, matched only by dizzying highs that brought nose bleeds. I would start the 60s a relative unknown and end the decade co-starring with America's favorite dog.

But I'm getting ahead of myself ...

1960, in particular, would begin with my first trip to the Great White Way, and end with the birth of my first son. Not bad for an "under-fiver" who only a year earlier had resorted to stealing suits and driving drunks around Manhattan to make ends meet.

Not bad at all ...

Viva Madison Avenue

My first thoughts as I got off the phone with my new agent, Lionel Larner, were, "I can't believe it. Broadway. I didn't have to wait as long as I thought, after all ..."

The show was called *Viva Madison Avenue* and, according to my agent, would be starring some of the biggest names in live theater, among them Buddy Hackett and Marty Balsam.

And, best of all, Jed Allan as "the Stag," a pencil pushing stud at the advertising agency, Lowell & Lynch, around which the play by George Panetta revolved. Scheduled for an early April opening, there was just enough time to assemble the cast and begin rehearsal at the famed Longacre Theatre on West 48th Street.

I had auditioned weeks earlier, and after getting the call could hardly contain my enthusiasm. Toby was so cute. She was so proud of me, and knew how much I wanted to be on Broadway. We had little time to celebrate, however, as rehearsals would be starting right away.

Broadway was not new to me. After all, my father had played in orchestra pits up one side of that fabled street and down the other for years and, as many times as not, I'd tagged along as often as I could. But stepping onto a Broadway stage for the first time as a paid performer? I've got to tell you, I just couldn't wait.

Unfortunately, there was trouble from the very beginning …

Meeting the Cast

Things started out smoothly enough with our first few script readings in New York. The cast up to this point seemed to get along fine, and our first director, Ira Cirker, moved those initial read-throughs along despite Buddy Hackett's bawdy humor and wicked asides to his fellow actors, most of whom were more interested in putting on a top-notch play than schmoozing with Buddy.

The son of a Brooklyn upholsterer, chubby-faced comic actor Buddy Hackett was no stranger to Broadway, having starred for two years in the comedy *Lunatics and Lovers*. He went on to play the title role in 1956 TV sitcom *Stanley* and, two years later, became a regular on Jackie Gleason's Saturday night variety series.

I didn't know what to make of this slapstick comic's blustery personality, except to note that the famous comic, who had reportedly once turned down an offer to play "Curly" in *The Three Stooges*, was doing his best to "dirty up" what was essentially a sweet, moving piece by playwright George Panetta, who had written the earlier play *Comic Strip* to some success and was thus trying to beat the "sophomore jinx" with this, his second play.

Even in those first few read-throughs, I could see the writing on the wall and soon the sophomore writer was taking notes from Buddy. But while creative differences between the playwright, director, and star of stage and screen simmered, I took the time to get to know several of my co-stars.

I had been a huge fan of the enormously famous Martin "Marty" Balsam since seeing him in 1954's *On the Waterfront* and later in 1957's *12 Angry Men*. Though he would later go on to even greater fame, one might say infamy, playing the cynical, skeptical private detective Arbogast in Alfred Hitchcock's *Psycho*, for now he was returning to his first love, the stage, and I couldn't have been more proud to share it with him.

Fred Clark, playing Ed Noone, was another familiar face. After all, I'd watched the bald, dour character actor as the pompous neighbor Harry Morton on *The George Burns and Gracie Allen Show* for years. In person, he turned out to be one of the funniest, sweetest, and kindest actors I'll ever have the privilege of working with. I only wish that you all could have been so lucky to know the man as I was.

A wonderful teacher and actor by the name of Paul E. Richards was marvelous as our "Toro" in *Viva Madison Avenue*, while a young, attractive actress named Frances Sternhagen rounded out our principle cast as Buddy Hackett's secretary, "Dee Jones."

Now you can catch her playing what I like to call such "granny parts" as Virginia McCain in Stephen King's *Misery* or more recently as Marge Murray in the HBO Film *The Laramie Project*, but back when I first met her Frances was a sturdy stage veteran who was still in her teens when she made her first professional stage appearance in a 1948 summer-stock production of *The Glass Menagerie*.

Such were the members of my "Broadway family" for the duration …

Murder, Inc.

Reputed mob boss Albert Anastasia, a.k.a. "The Mad Hatter" or the "Lord High Executioner" succeeded Vincent Mangano as one of the most high-profile bosses of the Gambino crime family. Along with other enforcers, the ruthless executioner of some of the 50s biggest crime figures killed for fun and profit under the underworld banner "Murder, Inc."

Albert Anastasia's own reign of terror ended, as it had begun, with murder; he was gunned down by two men in a barber shop in the lobby of the Park Sheraton Hotel. No one was ever arrested for the crime.

Why even bring any of this up? I really don't know, except for the fact that, in a strange twist of fate, Buddy Hackett actually lived in Anastasia's old house in Fort Lee, New Jersey.

Then again, perhaps it wasn't fate that found Hackett living in the old headquarters of Murder, Inc., but ego instead. The impressive mansion was a place that Buddy loved to brag about and, more importantly, show off. For years buddy had been inviting his comedian cronies back to the house after yet another round of golf at the country club they all belonged to in Englewood, New Jersey.

But now the sprawling old house became the setting for many of our "cast parties" after those long days of rehearsal. Though it was far from my style, I was always intrigued by "the Anastasia house." It was big and brooding, full of all kinds of spiraling staircases, winding hallways, and a ton of nooks and crannies.

In short, it was exactly the house you'd expect from a bunch of guys trying to hide shit from the police. But there was no use trying to hide the pride in Buddy's face every time the cast was invited over to hob knob with the rich and famous.

I'll never forget the time I turned around and was suddenly facing Sidney Poitier at one of Hackett's "Anastasia" parties. I had long looked up to and idolized Mr. Poitier as an actor with style and class. Hearing that instantly recognizable voice say, "Hello" was the thrill of a lifetime. But running into him at a casual evening affair at the house of one of my co-stars was just one of the many high points of the beginning of the 1960s.

Rehearsals

Since Broadway is the standard, the gold seal, for live performances, few shows ever truly "premiere" on the Great White Way without a few hard kicks of the tires first. Instead, they are often taken for long "test drives" out on the road, often in nearby towns such as Boston, Philadelphia, or Connecticut.

Such was the case with *Viva Madison Avenue*. By this point we had lost our first director, Ira Cirker, due to "creative differences" with the show's producer, Martin H. Poll, and its star, Buddy Hackett. To my dismay, Cirker was quickly replaced with the show's second director, Aaron Frankel, who I'd already found to be rather weak and ineffectual from our time together on *Tiger at the Gates* back at Bucks County Playhouse.

Still, I was thrilled to be going to Broadway and eager for a smooth road trip as we settled into the famed Forrest Theater in Philly. So far I'd formed fast friendships with the other cast members and a grudging respect for its diminutive but dynamic star, Buddy Hackett.

Until the day he crossed the line, that is. On the afternoon in question, Hackett, Balsam, and I were sitting center stage during rehearsals in Philly with the rest of the cast and crew seated in the first three rows as we read our lines.

I don't quite remember the scene, but I do remember "his highness" Mr. Hackett was seated in a throne of some sort, which certainly must have pleased him to no end. We were reading through a scene we'd no doubt rehearsed ad nauseum by now, but for some reason Buddy grew incensed after I delivered one of my lines. Despite the fact that I'd been delivering it the same way, at the same time, for over three weeks by now.

"Hey kid," he interrupted the scene in his inimitable way, spitting not-so-constructive criticism through the side of his overly verbose mouth, "What the hell are you doing? You just walked on my funniest line!"

I wasn't the only one flabbergasted in the wake of Hackett's hatchet job. You could have heard a pin drop as I tried to do damage control by apologizing as best I could, despite my wounded ego. "I'm sorry, Buddy," I said, even in my embarrassment refusing to call him Mr. Hackett. "I didn't know—"

"You don't know is right, kid, you don't know what the hell you're doing," Buddy began before continuing to cut me down in front of any and all assembled, in other words the whole cast.

Unfortunately, that was only the beginning of the day's abuse …

Somehow I managed to keep my anger in check and we resumed the scene. On the very next line, however, which just happened to be one of my funniest lines of the piece, just as I was about to deliver it, Mr. Hackett sits up in his chair and gooses himself on the arm of his throne!

I was, to say the least, fucking apoplectic.

Buddy Hackett or no, no one tells me that I don't know what I'm doing, even if I *don't* know what I'm doing. If that doesn't make sense, tough! Rising up from my seat to tower over the portly actor, still sitting impotently in his stage throne, I asked him point blank in a thundering voice that reached all the way to the back of the darkened theater, "What the fuck are you doing? You just reamed me out in front of all these people because I stepped on one of your shitty lines? Then you turn around and step on *my* line? Who the fuck do you think you are?"

In the midst of a growing verbal battle, a dignified Marty Balsam quickly walked off the set entirely. "I'm out of here," he said as he exited, stage left. Or was it right? "If you don't like it, call my agent…"

Some of the cast and crew thought Marty might have left the show entirely. I didn't think so, he was much too professional for that, but I was just as eager as they were to get to the bottom of it. As luck would have it, it was time for a break anyway and, as lunch was called, I went out looking for him.

I found Marty having a quiet drink in a restaurant called the Harvey House, where we all used to hang out. "Marty, what are you doing?" I asked as I joined him at his quiet table for two. "People think you walked off the show."

As I suspected, he hadn't walked off the show, just the stage. "I can't just walk off the show," he insisted. "I just couldn't take the noise anymore." He eventually calmed me down and, later that day, we both returned to the set no worse for the wear.

On the way back into the theater he quietly assured me, "Don't worry, kid. Buddy will apologize…"

I said, "Bull."

He just smiled and said, "Wait, you'll see …"

Sure enough, he did.

Well, sort of …

A week later, as we all gathered onstage for our daily reading, Marty still hadn't arrived yet. Buddy whispered to me out of the side of his mouth, "Hey, kid, let's make this work …"

Not quite an apology, but he *was* trying and, anyway, I *wanted* it to work. Afterward, a nervous silence filled the theater as we all wondered where Mr. Balsam was. Moments later, the mystery was solved when the new director, Aaron Frankel, made an announcement: "Buddy and I and the producers thought Marty wasn't quite right for the role… and his understudy is taking over." Since we sort of made up, I immediately looked at Buddy and asked, "Did you say that?"

Out of the side of his mouth he assured me that, "I didn't say that." Then, just as quickly, he said to our director, "Hey, Aaron, I never said Marty wasn't right for the show."

Stammering, Frankel amended his original statement with a quick, "Well, the *producers* and I thought Marty wasn't quite right for the role." Still, the betrayed look on his face just about gave the true story away.

Then again, perhaps we'll never know the truth about that …

Fred Clark leaned toward me and admitted, "I thought *you* were gonna be fired …"

I said, "So did I …"

It Must Have Been the Flanken

Several days before we were scheduled to return to New York for our Broadway premiere, Buddy Hacket, my understudy, and I went for a quick lunch at Rosa's Deli just across from the Forrest Theater.

Tensions had eased somewhat between Buddy and myself, though I still didn't trust him and, if I hadn't been so hungry, might not have chosen to break bread with him in the first place. Still, we'd all been together so long by now it was like a family: You may not always like each other, but you stick together.

Sometimes, however, that's easier said than done …

On this particular day Abe, our geriatric Jewish waiter, was carrying the tray that seemed to have been surgically attached to his withered hand and walking on the heels of his feet, as was his habit. (He was about eighty-five years old.)

It's a funny thing I've noticed about old Jewish waiters over the years: As long as they're still breathing—and can still hold a tray, of course—the owners keep them on. Abe came over to take our order, starting, as always, with Buddy's. "What can I get you today, Mr. Hackett?" he asked, stooped from age but eternally star struck.

"I want a piece of flanken with no fat, and no potatoes," Buddy ordered officiously, barely looking up from his menu. Now, for you gentiles out there, flanken is the Hebrew word for brisket, which is technically a strip of beef from the chuck end of the short ribs. In other words, it's nothing *but* fat. In essence, ordering flanken with no fat is like ordering spareribs … with no ribs.

Naturally, delivering the impossible would have been hard enough for any waiter, but minutes later poor Abe limped over to our table proudly bearing a typical piece of flanken, heavy on the fat, and a typical side dish, one potato. "I hope you like this, Mr. Hackett," said Abe kindly, setting the plate before his idol.

"What is this?" spat Hackett, his ire growing by degrees. "I asked for a piece of flanken, *no* fat, and *no* potato. I've got a fatty piece of flanken *and* a potato. What the hell is wrong with you?"

"Well, Mr. Hackett," stammered Abe by way of apology, "You know what I think the best thing for you is …"

"You know what's best for me, Charlie? No advice," said Buddy before our geriatric waiter could finish. Now, he knew as well as I did that our waiter's name was Abe, but "Charlie" was Buddy's term for just about everybody. Especially when he was demeaning them. "Now I'm going to the can, and when I come back there better be a leaner piece of flanken on my plate … and no potato."

With that, the star of *Viva Madison Avenue* waddled off to the men's room. I don't know what Abe brought Mr. Hackett that day, nor what he dished up for me, for that matter. I certainly wasn't sticking around to find out.

As my understudy made excuse after excuse for Buddy's rude behavior, I grabbed my coat and left a few bills on the table to cover my lunch, whatever it might be. I was no longer hungry. "You make all the excuses you want," I said as I left, "but start with this one. Tell 'Mr. Hackett' that I had a stomachache. It must have been the flanken …"

The Show Goes On

Several weeks and nine cast changes later, *Viva Madison Avenue* finally opened on April 6, 1960 at the Longacre Theatre, without its first director and without Marty Balsam. It was my first live performance on the Great White Way and exhilarating for a number of reasons, one of which was the reaction I got my first time walking onstage.

My entrance onto the Great White Way was inside a phone booth, but even my elaborate set dressing didn't shield me from the harsh glare of those beaming stage lights, nor from an apparently adoring audience.

Apparently, playing "the Stag," a not-so-hidden reference to "the stud," was a tight bit of type-casting because, as a big twenty-four-year-old stepping onto stage in a suit—not stolen—but great looking all the same at the start of my very first show on Broadway, the audience let out an audible, "Oooooooh…"

Whether it was out of fright or trepidation I could not know at the time, but my first thought was that, perhaps, my fly was unzipped. Why else would they "oooooh" like that? Hesitating before uttering my first line, I surreptitiously checked and, amazingly, my fly was, in fact, zipped. I breathed a sigh of relief. After all, in the famous words of David Niven when a streaker had run behind him at the 1973 Oscars ceremony, I didn't want the audience to see my shortcomings.

"Didn't you hear the audience gasp?" asked a fellow cast member after the first act.

"Yeah," I said, thinking nothing of it. "I thought my fly was open!"

"That was for you, you dummy," he said.

The second reason my first night on Broadway was memorable came as a result of a standing ovation that went on *behind* the scenes ....

Despite the ups and downs of our Philadelphia performances, the show's producer, Martin H. Poll, had been impressed with my performance as "The Stag." So much so that he had called his good friend and Hollywood agent Henry Willson, on my behalf.

Willson was the man behind such screen legends as Troy Donahue, Tab Hunter, and Guy Madison. He also had another client whose real name, Roy Fitzgerald, was changed by combining the "Rock of Gibraltar" and the "Hudson River" to come up with the name for biggest client, Rock Hudson.

Just before our first performance, Marty told me that Mr. Willson was coming to New York to "see the show" and would like to meet me. According to Marty, he had told Mr. Willson all about me and insisted, "You gotta come and meet this guy."

Mr. Willson had agreed and, now that our first performance was in the bag, I was eager to see him make good on his promise. Unfortunately, big Hollywood agents weren't the only ones coming to see the show.

That first night, several prominent critics for the only papers that mattered had been in the audience, and hadn't taken too kindly to Buddy's "weak attempts at comedy," or his "trying too hard to be funny" and especially not his "dirtying up" of what was essentially a straightforward comedy meant for family audiences.

In short, the reviews were horrible …

On the lam …

Word spreads quickly on Broadway, and bad first night reviews can only mean one thing: No second night. Still, by Equity standards producers are supposed to give all performers twenty-four hour notice of a show's closing, and I basically "hid out" after the first show so that there could at least be a second.

I wasn't alone. When I reported for duty that second night, turns out several other cast members had been "on the lam" as well so that we could get that all-important second performance out of our system.

Of course, I had another agenda and was desperate for Henry Willson to see the show before it closed. Unfortunately, that was not to be. After only two performances, *Viva Madison Avenue* closed its doors.

At the wrap party, I was hesitant to ask Marty if Mr. Willson was still coming to "see me," especially since there was no longer any show to see me in.

"Sure kid," said Marty. "He'll be in town next week. My secretary will call you when he gets into town and set up an appointment. Don't worry, kid, he'll be here."

Sure enough, several days later Marty's secretary called and set up an appointment with the legendary Hollywood talent agent. The next day I arrived at his suite at the Pierre Hotel.

Please, Spell the Name Right

I was ushered into a sumptuous penthouse by Mr. Willson's then boy-friend, a "man" my age but as pretty as any woman I'd ever seen. Mr. Willson was lounging in a spacious office suite and, before even saying "Hello," he exclaimed, "My God, you've got big feet! Rock's a size twelve, how big are … yours?"

I wasn't so naive and the implication was clear, but I wasn't offended because, after all, it was close.

"Well," I said, "mine are only an eleven and a half, but I hope that won't hold me back."

Apparently, it was the right response. After several minutes of talking and letting him know where I'd been and what I'd done, Mr. Willson of-fered to represent me. "I want you to come out to California. I'll make you a big star."

I could hardly believe my ears. Rock Hudson's agent wanted to sign me. "California?" I asked, uncertain. "When?"

"How about a month?" he asked. "Will that be long enough to get your affairs in order?"

Hardly, I thought to myself. As a matter of fact, my affairs had recently become quite complicated. "I don't know if I can do that, Mr. Willson," I explained, much to his chagrin. "I just got started out here, my first show on Broadway was last week and I really want to be a stage actor. Besides that well, I just learned … my wife is expecting," I tripped over the words, still getting used to them myself.

Toby had announced just after we'd returned to New York and were preparing to open the show that she was, in fact, pregnant. I couldn't have been more pleased, but Mr. Willson didn't quite seem to share my enthusi-asm.

"I don't know what the future holds," he explained. "I'd love to work with you, but I need you on the West Coast. I'm in film and that's where they make 'em. I'd still love to handle you, so when you're ready to make the switch from stage to screen, please come and see me."

With that, I bid the biggest agent in Hollywood goodbye.

At least for now …

Jed Allan

Taxi Cab Confessions, Take 2

Words can't describe how heartbroken I was with the closing of my first Broadway show, nor how crushed I felt to be a working actor on Friday and, by that following Monday, an out of work actor.

With no prospects, it was back to driving a cab. I didn't want to do it but driving a taxi around Manhattan was the one job that allowed me the freedom, not to mention the proximity, to go on theater auditions. That was why I was the best dressed cab driver in all of Manhattan. On any given day I could have an audition or get a call back, so I always had to be ready in one of my illicit suits.

With a child on the way, Toby and I needed the money more than ever, and so late in 1961 I got back in a checkered cab and began driving through the streets of New York. The days were long and the nights were longer, but I was doing what I had to do and that was all that mattered.

Then again, some people could have cared less …

One evening during the intermission between the first and second acts at some long forgotten Broadway show, I was steering through traffic on East 45th street right outside of the Belasco Theater.

Traffic was congested and made even more so by the putz in the car in front of me who wouldn't move his car as he gawked at all the sharp looking ladies standing around in their evening gowns and pearls.

"Hey, buddy," I thought, "I'm looking too but I can drive at the same time."

When repeated epithets, hand gestures, and horn honks failed to have the desired result and the guy's car was still in front of me after several minutes, I did what all professional cab drivers in Manhattan do when the car in front of them won't get the message: I bumped into his rear bumper. Now who's the putz?

Immediately the other putz was out of the driver's seat and looking for my face to hit. He did. I did. We both did. Including the second guy in the car, the one I didn't see.

Suddenly, a bystander shouted, "Wait a minute!" and, assuming he was there to break up the fight I paused just before he concluded his sentence, "Lemme hit him!"

Down I went with the sucker punch and, once down, next came more punches and even a few kicks as I tried in vain to shield my head. That was the last thing I remember before waking up in an ambulance ready to leave for Roosevelt Hospital.

"Hey buddy," said an innocent bystander who handed me the money I'd had in pocket of the jacket I'd formerly had, which was now useless, "you were doing okay until that other guy showed up."

The doctors at the hospital patched me up, but they couldn't do anything about my favorite black blazer, which had been ripped to shreds during the altercation. Patched up and taped together, they released me that night and before I left the hospital I called Toby to tell her what had happened.

"Toby darling," I muttered through sore teeth, "I'm sorry I'm late but I'm on my way home. I had a fight and a little problem. I'm getting my car and coming home. I swear. I'll be home in about forty-five minutes."

Of course, I had to take a taxi back to the garage to pick up my own car, and then drive home to our apartment in Rego Park, Queens. When Toby saw me looking like a walking Frankenstein, she burst into tears.

I would later learn that there were two reasons for the tears. "They really did a number on you," she said as she tenderly traced the bandages and tape covering my face and head after I told her the whole story. "But that's not the only reason I'm crying."

"What's the other reason?" I asked innocently.

"I melted all of your favorite .45 records!" she admitted.

Somehow between her sobbing—and mine—I learned that, while doing some winter cleaning, Toby had set the cardboard box containing all of my precious .45s on the radiator, forgetting it as the heat came on until the smell of melting wax became instantly recognizable. By then, of course, it was too late …

All of my original recordings put on .45s of Benny Goodman and Glen Miller were gone, forever, but I could hardly get mad as I reassured a still crying Toby that, "It's okay, I can replace them…"

That was surely a night to remember.

Or, perhaps, a night to forget …

Jed Allan

Happy Birthday, Mitch!

Mitchell Seth Brown was born on December 23, 1960, and Toby and I couldn't have been prouder. We'd come a long way since she'd tricked me, ehhr, proposed to me on that sultry summer night in my father's car, and now we were married.

With child …

To my complete consternation, and perpetual embarrassment, Mitch was but one of two sons I would miss seeing being born, though to my credit it was never my fault. Well, not entirely.

When Toby's contractions started, she and her dutiful husband went straight to the hospital where, as was often the case in those days, the doctor told us that she would not give birth for "at least four to five hours."

And why would a doctor lie? So, as was also the practice in that day, I rushed home for a quick cat nap, figuring I'd have plenty of time to witness the miracle of birth after getting some quick sack time. An hour and a half later I returned to the hospital and there was Toby. Smiling. Radiant.

Glowing.

And holding our beautiful baby boy …

Seems our doctor had been off by about, oh, say, four to five hours. Several years later I would make a repeat performance of missing the birth of my middle son, Dean, but that's a whole other story …

We returned from the hospital to our new apartment in Queens, surrounded by family and friends. The apartment was much better than our previous digs in the basement of the nudist winery, and seemed a fitting place to raise a family with its sunken living room and bright, airy windows.

The responsibility of fatherhood weighed heavily on me, but was offset by the joy little Mitch brought to the growing Allan family. As Mitch grew he would show a talent for the "family business," landing two pilots and a thirteen-week run on a series called *The Cowboys*, based on the John Wayne movie, as a kid before "quitting the business" for good.

Well, not for good; for eight years while his braces straightened his teeth out. Then a couple of more years of trying, and *then* he quit.

Mitch had a problem. He was great as an actor; he was even better as a singer. But every time he performed on stage as a singer, he froze. He was deathly afraid of performing in front of other people, *any* people, and, even as a young child, used to only sing to his mother if he could do it standing behind a door … so she couldn't see him. He improved his performing level somewhat, but not enough for him to be comfortable.

Which was too bad, because he has a voice like a bird … to this day.

I only wish he had listened to me a little more closely about his career options because there have been so many performers over the years who were dead weight on stage, yet had a marvelous career as "recording artists" because they had wonderful voices and could truly shine in the studio. To be a giant in the business, you still had to perform in front of an audience; that scared him to death.

These days my "little Mitch" has two kids of his own, Katie, nine, and Jake, eleven. But back then he was our little bundle of joy and brought a new sense of family to our first real apartment.

Not to mention a new sense of urgency to my job search …

"Thank You" Meant "Goodbye"

1961 began with uncertainty as Toby stayed home to care for Mitch and I hit the bricks looking for work. Somehow we muddled through the spring and summer with freelance work and the occasional "under five" role, but as winter came to the city I found an open call listing in a popular trade paper called *Dramalogue* for a new musical called *All-American*, to star the inimitable Ray Bolger as a college professor from Europe who discovers the melting pot of America.

Based on a book by Mel Brooks with lyrics by Lee Adams and music by Charles Strouse, the show was to be directed by Tony winner Joshua Logan and would also star Anita Gillette as Susan, Eileen Herlie as Elizabeth Hawkes-Bullock, Ron Husmann as Edwin Bricker and Fritz Weaver as Henderson.

I desperately wanted a role, any role, and called my agent to ask him for advice.

"Wear tight pants," was all he said, in deference to the director's passion for virile young men.

Jed Allan

Arriving the day of the casting call, tight pants painted firmly on, I quickly found myself competing for a spot in the chorus, which was a standard part of any Broadway musical at that time.

The audition consisted of 100 guys standing on stage at the same time, most of them conspicuously wearing pants as tight as mine. The stage manager would call out "Number One, please" and victim number one would step forward to sing eight bars of whatever song he'd rehearsed. Afterward the director would say "Thank you" before the stage manager would yell "Next!" again to repeat the system all over again.

"Thank you" meant "goodbye" …

Occasionally, however, Logan would like what he heard and, in between a dozen shouts of "Next!" you would hear, "Thank you, would you wait a minute please?" before the stage manager screamed "Next!" again.

I was one of the fortunate tight-pants clad young men who was favored with a brusque, "Thank you, would you wait a minute, please?" After a dozen or so of us who had been told to wait a minute watched the stage clear of those less fortunate then ourselves, we were granted a private audience with the director.

"What have you done?" asked Josh Logan when it was my turn.

Among other credits, I settled on *Under the Yum Yum Tree*, adding, "…and I was better than Dean Jones," hoping to sound confident.

"So what?" Logan shot back. "So were a lot of people …"

Despite his retort, however, I later got the job and Logan himself told me once the cast had been assembled that he'd hired me because he thought I'd been "ballsy."

Well, what did he expect?

It's hard to be anything else in tight pants besides, my voice was getting higher.

Straight Guy in the Chorus

Rehearsals for *All-American* began in high winter at a New York rehearsal hall and, perhaps it was the search for body heat that led some of the male dancers in the chorus to search for companionship … amongst themselves.

Please, Spell the Name Right

Occasionally, however, they went too far and looked for it with me …

The name *All-American* was a play on words, blending the melting pot theme of the American experience with the All-American game of football. Thus the entire chorus was dressed like football players, while half of us sang and the other half danced.

Fortunately or not, I was a better dancer than most of the singers, so I was put on the dancing football team, as opposed to the singer team. I use those words, fortunately or not, because every time we got into a huddle, I got goosed.

Usually it was impossible to tell who had goosed you, since dancers move pretty quickly. One day, however, I turned just in time to see a dancer named Bob Loan take a chunk out of my ass and, after rehearsal was through, pinned him against a wall backstage. "If you ever do that again," I warned him, "I'll break that finger and shove it up *your* ass!"

Though he seemed to like the idea, I was nonetheless never goosed again …

Working Out the Kinks

Best known for his role as the Scarecrow in *The Wizard of Oz*, Ray Bolger was a gentle soul whose talent was eclipsed only by his insecurity. This was never more evident than as we began to perform for live audiences in Connecticut.

So afraid was Ray that the audiences might not come back after intermission, he used to keep them in their seats, literally, by performing between the first and second acts. Not only was this unheard of for live stage performances, but with good reason: It meant the orchestra rarely got a break.

Ray had had a huge stage hit with *Where's Charly?* a George Abbott adaptation of the comedy *Charley's Aunt* back in the 50s. Heralded for his singing as much as his performance in that play, Bolger's legacy lived on in the hit song, "Once in Love with Amy":

For once in love with Amy,
Always in love with Amy,

Jed Allan

Ever and ever fascinated by her,
Sets your heat a-fire to stay.

And so, during intermission, both his fellow actors and the audience were treated to a nightly rendition of his hit, "Once in Love with Amy." Talk about singing for your supper!

George Lindsey was another young actor in *All-American*, though you may know him best as "Goober" from the television series *The Andy Griffith Show*. But what you might not know was that the actor who went on to be known as America's favorite "lovable hick" actually has a Bachelors Degree in BioScience from the University of Alabama and was a science teacher before deciding to become an actor. He also had a young boy of his own, who had been born only a few months before Mitch. Not surprisingly, we became close—and long-lasting—friends.

Rounding out the cast were stage veterans Eileen Herlie, who has had the distinction of playing Queen Gertrude opposite two on-screen Hamlets: Laurence Olivier in 1948, and Richard Burton in 1964, and Fritz Weaver, who debuted on Broadway in 1955's *The Chalk Circle*. Ron Husmann had recently been nominated for a Tony Award for Best Featured Actor in a Musical for his work in *Tenderloin*, while Anita Gillette had recently been awarded the 1960 Theatre World Awards Theatre World Award for her work in Russell Patterson's *Sketchbook*.

All in all, I'd say I was in good company …

The Face of Censorship

Being in the chorus of a star-studded show like *All-American* may have been a boost for my career, but certainly didn't do wonders for my ego. With two lines, I could hardly be called a principle.

But, little did I know, my script would be cut in half …

One of my lines, which just so happened to be one of the play's funniest lines, came in the first act as I played a traffic cop to Ray Bolger's doddering old man. As I'm standing there in full regalia, whistle in hand, busily directing "traffic" center stage, Ray's character comes up and asks, "Excuse me, officer, but do you know where I can get a bus?"

Please, Spell the Name Right

Frustrated, gruff, and impatient, like any typical traffic copy would respond, I say gruffly, "You're gonna get one right in the ass if you don't get up on the sidewalk!"

Shakespeare? Hardly. But it killed every night in New Haven. I always looked forward to saying it because it was a guaranteed laugh.

Unfortunately, days before we were to leave Connecticut and return to Broadway to embark upon our opening night, a humble and abashed Ray Bolger approached me backstage and asked, "Would you mind taking one of your lines out?"

Flabbergasted, I responded the only way I knew how, "But Mr. Bolger, I only have two!"

Apparently Ray's wife thought the line was "too dirty" and had asked the husband to ask the chorus boy if he could lose the line. Out of respect for Ray, I did.

Like I had a choice …

Truth be known, I think he felt that the line made fun of him. Or his wife did, anyway. Who knows. Who cares. It only bothered me for a little while. Forty years, I guess, 'cause I'm still talking about it!

My First (and last) Brush with the Paparazzi

Just before my second Broadway play was to open in New York, a milestone of another sort occurred on Florida's "space coast." On February 20, 1962, astronaut John Glenn piloted the Mercury-Atlas 6 "Friendship 7" spacecraft on the first manned orbital mission of the United States.

Launched from Kennedy Space Center, Florida, he completed a successful three-orbit mission around the earth, reaching a maximum altitude of approximately 162 miles and an orbital velocity of approximately 17,500 miles per hour.

As a result, the country in general, and our leading man in particular, was riding the current wave of patriotism. Accordingly, at the end of each show we were forced to stand in line for the traditional bows and wave American flags instead.

As the tallest member of the chorus, I was always the last in line and bordered on hovering between backstage and onstage at the end of every performance. One night as I took my place in line and waved my little flag, I heard the unmistakable sound of someone whispering "Pssst!"

At first I thought it was a fellow cast member, warning me that my fly was open again, but after glancing down the row of beaming faces to my left I saw no one looking my way. Hearing the "Pssst!" sound once again, though this time growing louder, I looked into the audience just in time to see a woman doing a duck walk down the aisle and holding a camera.

It was my mother …

"I think I've got a problem," I said to myself.

Camera firmly in hand, she was bound and determined to get a shot of her son on Broadway. Now, everyone knows you can't take pictures in a Broadway theater. Everyone except my mom. Before I could stop her from committing Cardinal Live Theater Sin # 1, away she snapped, her Saltine sized flashbulb sending a lightning glare across the entire stage.

Naturally, the unnatural lighting caught the eye of the show's star and, after glancing in my direction and seeing the infraction in progress, Mr. Bolger dutifully recognized the impassioned zeal of a proud mother and, instead of firing me, he and the whole cast applauded.

My first ovation.

Or was it my mother's?

Either way, my mother, Celia Brown, was at once my best and worst publicist ever. Once she fainted at a busy lunch counter and, upon being roused, a good Samaritan asked my mother if she was okay. When she nodded her head yes, the man naturally asked if she knew her name.

My mother responded like any good publicist would, "My name is Celia Brown and my son's name is Jed Allan. Would you like to see his picture?!?" To this day her zeal goes unmatched in the annals of celebrity mothers, and God rest her sweet soul, her first and last thought was always to further her son's career.

A Star is Born

Before I forget, while *All-American* completed its three-month run, in Philadelphia now, another popular show was starting at the same time, and destined to become much more memorable, if only for the introduction of a talented songbird the likes of which few in live theater had ever seen.

Based on the book by Jerome Weidman, with music and lyrics by Harold Rome, *I Can Get It for You Wholesale* was a musical comedy set in New York's garment district. Starring Lillian Roth, Marilyn Cooper, and Elliott Gould, the play featured a show stopping number called "Miss Marmelstein":

Miss Marmelstein! Miss Marmelstein! Miss Marmelstein!

Oh, why is it always Miss Marmelstein?

Miss Marmelstein? Miss Marmelstein?

Other girls get called by their first names right away

They get cozy intimate ... Do you know what I mean?

Sung by none other than Barbara Streisand herself, the number was quickly putting the otherwise lackluster play on the map and, though I could never get to the show in time to hear it, I could always count on seeing the show's two youngest principles, Gould and Streisand, at the popular Variety Club in Philadelphia during try-outs.

Often I would get there just in time to hear the show's frustrated director, Arthur Laurents, screaming at Streisand that she was "ruining his show!" You wonder how he ever became a director. Later, I would often ride the train home with Streisand, who lived in Jackson Heights, Queens, at the time never, I'm sorry to say, really getting to know her.

Oliver!

The Winter Garden Theatre was home to *All-American* from March 19, 1961 to May 26 of the same year. The show had garnered many of its stars great reviews, and even a popular melody that would soon become a major hit for none other than Tony Bennett, "Once Upon A Time," with words by Lee Adams and Music by Charles Strouse:

Once upon a time a girl with moonlight in her eyes

Put her hand in mine and said she loved me so

But that was once upon a time, very long ago ...

But as summer dawned on Broadway our show closed and, once again, I was out of work. It was well into 1962 by now but I was still having trouble with my nose as a result of that altercation on the night I got sucker punched, sent to the hospital, and vowed to never drive a cab again.

With a little extra money in my pocket from *All-American*, I was able to go to the hospital and get my nose put back to where it was before that fight with those two guys I "bumped into" while driving a cab.

After the procedure, my eyes were black and blue and I was bandaged for days. I was in such bad shape I had to stay at the hospital, and we could only afford a semi-private room. In those days, the rooms had no phones, at least not the cheap ones, and so whenever I got a call, which wasn't all that often, the nurse had to come get me.

One day the nurse approached with a message, "Mr. Allan, a man named Neil Hartley is on the phone for you. He called the nurse's station and we gave him the number to one of the pay phones in the hall. Would you like to take it?"

Out of work and restless, I would have talked to just about anybody at that point, even someone I'd never heard of before. When I answered the phone, however, it turned out that Neil Hartley was the right hand man for none other than the Tony award winning producer David Merrick, of *A Taste of Honey*, *Look Back in Anger*, and *Cactus Flower* fame.

After hasty introductions, Mr. Hartley told me about a new musical they were bringing over from England based on a book by Charles Dickens featuring Georgia Brown, Clive Revell, and Danny Sewell called *Oliver!* "Would I be interested?" he asked.

When I eloquently responded, "Are you putting me on?" he chuckled.

"I'm calling a phone booth in a hospital to reach you, would I be putting you on?" he asked.

"I'm grateful," I said, "thank you."

Next, he agreed to set up an audition and I innocently asked, "I have to audition for another chorus job? I just finished one…"

"No," he said, chuckling again. "I want you to understudy for the role of Bill Sykes."

"When?" I asked immediately, chomping at the bit.

He answered, "This week," and, though I could barely stand upright, I agreed. Now, for all those who never saw, or perhaps read, *Oliver!*, Bill Sykes is probably the most evil character in English fiction this side of Jack the Ripper.

And, since I was already a mess anyway, looking horrible wasn't going to be much of a problem for me. Already looking like "a bad guy," I took advantage of my poor "punim," which included bruised eyes and a nose so sore I could barely breathe. Still, minutes after showing up at the audition I launched into a particularly rousing rendition of an already rousing song, "Live Till I Die":

I'm gonna live till I die

I'm gonna laugh stead of cry

I'm gonna take the town turn it upside down

I'm gonna live, live, live until I die …

Amazingly it worked and I was hired for my third Broadway show. Two weeks later when I finally showed up for the cast's first read-through, however, I almost lost it! By then I had healed and was back to my old self, which was apparently not pleasing to the show's Assistant Director, who stopped me as I strolled confidently toward the stage.

"Who the hell are you?" he asked.

"I'm Jed Allan," I announced proudly. "I'm here to understudy for Danny Sewell." Now Sewell was a boxer turned actor, and looked it. A tough guy with the broad, flat nose of a professional fighter, he was in his mid-thirties by the time he starred in *Oliver!* and, here I was, ten years younger with a fresh nose job.

"Have they seen you?" asked the AD with all seriousness.

"Yes," I said, growing exasperated. "I auditioned for them."

I then had to explain to him my situation and, after several conferences with the powers that be, was allowed to stay on. I was as grateful for the work as I was the introduction to two of my new co-stars, the first being Clive Revill, who was nominated for Tony Awards for his performance in Broadway's *Irma La Douce* and, later, *Oliver!*

But as impressed as I was with my male co-stars, I was even more so with the female lead, husky-voiced British singer and actress Georgia Brown.

Georgia was a beautiful, sexy Anna Magnani type, only Jewish and, with much in common, we hit it off "beautifully" as well.

It was a good thing I had to go home every night …

On the Road Again

Little did I know it, but *Oliver!* would be a tremendous commitment for both myself and my young family. The family musical was a first in many areas, most notably because instead of rehearsing and staging experimental performances in one town before returning to Broadway, we were the first to tour the entire country on a tour that would last six months and take us from San Francisco to Los Angeles to Detroit and Toronto before finally landing on Broadway.

It was a thrilling experience, made even more so by the fact that Toby and Mitch, now nearly one year old, would be joining me. Our first stop was in San Francisco, where Toby, Mitch, and I shared a second-floor walk-up right on Post Street with, Donald Goodman, the young boy playing The Artful Dodger and his sister. He was a good kid. It's a shame he got too big for the part and was replaced by Davy Jones.

Having Toby and Mitch along made the experience all the more rewarding, but occasionally frightening. Our long staircase downstairs was a particularly hazardous set-up, and so Toby and I dutifully installed a gate to keep little Mitch from getting out.

Unfortunately, Mitch had other ideas …

One morning a week or so into dress rehearsals I awoke to a loud banging on the front door at eight a.m. Startled, I rose to find an employee from the local gas station with whom I'd become friendly since arriving in town.

He was holding a smiling, giggling, naked Mitch …

"What are you doing with my son?" I asked.

"What am I doing with your son?" asked the good Samaritan. "Don't you keep an eye on your own kid? He was outside wandering around in the buff and managed to make it all the way down to my station before I snatched him up and brought him over here!"

Please, Spell the Name Right

The gas station was nearly a quarter of a block away …

Of Pitches, Pit Bulls & Performances

I got to play Bill Sykes for the first time as our whirlwind national tour finally swung through Detroit about three months in. Danny Sewell was out sick and I was "it" that night.

The evening was memorable for many things, particularly my performance, which went well, not to mention the acceptance of the cast, but also for the performance of the cast's resident pit bull.

The dog, whose name now escapes me but his letting out of a constant stream of gas never escaped me. The problem was, he saved his biggest oil reserves for a scene which centered around a bridge. A bridge all cast members had to cross. A bridge all cast members had to cross after said pit bull had passed … gas.

I wouldn't get to play Bill Sykes again until we got to Broadway, and even then it happened to be my fault. Sewell and I played together on the Broadway Show League baseball team.

Now being a former boxer Danny could knock you out with one punch, but it just so happens he couldn't play softball worth a damn, though. I sure thought he could. I threw him a ball once and, unfortunately, he caught it wrong.

He ended up breaking two fingers and the pain was so bad that he couldn't hold the club that his character used to hit people with. As a result, he couldn't perform for three nights. I felt really bad, ha ha ha. And so, for the next seventy-two hours, I *was* Billy Sykes, on Broadway, in one of the most popular musicals of all time.

If I didn't know myself any better, I might think I threw that ball on purpose.

Luckily Danny Sewell knew me even better than myself.

He never once blamed me for breaking his fingers …

The Equity Deputy Meets Manhattan Transfer

Oliver! was a play full of children and, in a play full of children … the "oldest kid is king." Or, in this case, The Equity Deputy. At twenty-four, by far the oldest of our "kids," it was my job to see that every person in the cast got his break on time, never worked a day too many, or even an extra hour, children especially. It wasn't always easy, but as an understudy I was making $185 a week at the time and was a part of one of Broadways' most successful musicals.

I enjoyed much success, both professionally and personally, with *Oliver!*, but after six months on the road and a year and a half in New York, I'd had enough. I was thinking about quitting. For one thing, there was talk of taking the show on the road for a second year and I just wasn't up for the travel.

Besides, something else was about to appear on the horizon.

Another son ...

Dean Stewart Brown was born on July 6, 1963.

"Was I there for the birth?" you might ask yourself.

"Of course not," I'd answer. At the time, I was doing a matinee and, by the time Toby had gone into labor I couldn't leave the stage to go to the hospital. And that old cliché? The one about "the show must go on?" Well, it went on all right. I did see her between shows, however. Toby looked beautiful, and so did my boy Dean.

He still does ...

Graciously, gratefully, I bowed out of *Oliver!* and returned to the life of a freelancer. I thought I had gotten to know many of the kids well that year I was with *Oliver*, but apparently not as well as some of the kids had gotten to know me.

Years later, in 1974, I attended a concert at the Roxy Theater in Los Angeles that blew me away. The group I saw that night was Manhattan Transfer and Toby and I liked them so much that I returned several nights later to buy tickets for ourselves and another couple, with whom we wanted to share this unique musical experience.

As I was standing in line waiting for the tickets, one of the group's four members approached me .. by name.

"Mr. Allan," he said humbly, as if, perhaps, he was there to buy tickets to see me instead of the complete opposite. "How are you?"

"Hey," I said enthusiastically, unaware of this talented young man's name. "I caught your act the other night and loved it so much I'm here to see it again and buy tickets for some friends of mine. But, if you don't mind me asking, how do you know me?"

"I followed your career for years," he responded, "you probably don't remember me, but I'm Allan Paul … I was the youngest kid in *Oliver!* I was twelve in 1962 and, since then, well, here I am…"

"You have just made me feel so old," I said.

We exchanged hugs and he asked me backstage after the show. I must say, being on Broadway has its perks …

The Under Fiver Meets 1963

So, 1963 found me walking away from one of Broadways' most successful musicals and entering the land of the freelance actor once again. I was a happily married husband, proud father, and Broadway veteran, but in spite of my impressive stage credits I soon found it rough going.

By hook or by crook I managed to find work in several films that year, including *Mirage* with Ernest Borgnine and Gregory Peck and another film called *Andy*, but if I wasn't an extra I was an "under fiver" and not much more.

I also found stage work in *12 Angry Men* with an idol of mine, Paul Muney, but as far as 1963 went, that was about it. It was one of those years in an actor's life when little seems to go well, professionally speaking, though I was able to enjoy more time than ever at home with Toby, Mitch, and Dean.

The year passed quickly. We were learning the actor's life. The ups. The downs. The in-betweens.

Unfortunately, this wasn't the ups.

Then again, it wasn't the downs, either.

Soon would come the mid-60s, when I would discover the joys, and sheer terror, of live television and my first soap operas. The 60s would also bring me my first series role working with an animal, and continued success on television and in various movies.

Though I didn't know it yet, 1963 was to be my last in between …

1964: IBM and Beyond …

Somehow Toby, the kids and I managed to muddle through a financially unstable 1963 and found ourselves smack dab in the middle of an equally turbulent 1964. Vietnam was a far distant land none of us had ever heard of before, but up to now 277 of our brave young soldiers had died, and over half of those casualties were from plane and helicopter crashes. As we all know, it got far, far worse. It never should have happened; we should not have been there.

Back on the home front, on the airwaves and spilling onto the city streets, The Beatles were everywhere and the so-called "British Invasion" had officially begun. Mod fashion swept the country and everywhere both boys and girls alike sported so-called "shag" hairdos.

Me? My style was more white tie and tails. The neat look. What am I talking about? No, I haven't lost it … yet. I'm referring to a phone call I got in early 1964 to be an emcee for the 1964–65 World's Fair, wearing a white tie and black tails and "warming up" an audience of nearly 500 each show. Out of work and running out of cash, I eagerly agreed, never imagining the grueling schedule I was setting myself up for as the show ran from April, 1964 through October of the same year.

Located on the same site as the 1939–40 New York World's Fair in Flushing Meadows, Queens, the theme for the mid-60s World's Fair was officially coined: "Peace Through Understanding." The unifying monument to this far-reaching theme was a twelve-story high, stainless-steel model of the earth known as the "Unisphere," around which the orbits of three satellites encircled this giant globe.

By the time this latest World's Fair ended in 1965 some 51 million people would have trampled its 650-acres, but my home for the duration would be the sleekly designed IBM Pavillion and rarely did I venture past its futuristic bounds, if only from sheer exhaustion.

Decked out in a full tuxedo, it was my job to emcee the futuristic theatrics of those brilliant minds at IBM. Ours was a popular exhibit, where a giant 500-seat grandstand was pushed by hydraulic rams high up into an ovoid-shaped rooftop theater. There, a nine-screen film showed the workings of computer logic.

Please, Spell the Name Right

In the middle of it all?

Yours truly …

Ten shows a day, twice on the hour, five hours a day, for sixteen straight weeks, I "worked the crowd" on a hydraulic pedestal that descended from the ceiling like something straight out of the Bat Cave. Dressed to the nines, I charmed the crowd with quick one-liners and even quicker ad-libs, all the while balancing myself on a moving stage designed by the folks who, decades later, would bring us into the computer age.

For now, it felt more like a torture rack …

Day after day, show after show, I would schmooze a crowd of up to 500 people as we were raised up and down like human pistons in a grand machine. After ten long minutes of what basically amounted to stand-up comedy, my pedestal would finally "land" and I would enjoy the dubious honor of lip-synching to the ten-minute film shown on a 180-screen that literally meant there wasn't a bad seat in the house.

Unfortunately, I was deemed "too funny" by IBM management. I always thought funny was good, like words starting with "K." But they felt I was distracting their audience from the Pavillion's main event, its ten-minute "commercial" for IBM products. As a result, I was summarily fired after sixteen straight weeks of near boot camp forced labor.

In the late 1970s, Flushing Meadows-Corona Park, as it is now called, became the home of the US Tennis Association and, in fact, the US Open tennis tournament is played there every year. The former New York City building is home to the Queens Museum of Art and continues to display the multi-million dollar model of the city of New York.

But for me, it will always hold fond, if exhausting, memories of a tuxedo clad young actor warming up an audience of 500 while he tried to keep his balance on a hydraulic lift that was far from the "stairway to heaven."

It might not have been the Beatles, but it was certainly my "Ticket to Ride" out those turbulent 60s with grace, poise, and enough pocket change to feed my growing family as we continued to navigate the ups and downs of an actor's gypsy lifestyle.

As I was quickly learning, that was what being a "working actor" was all about.

It was also called surviving …

Fool on the Hill

Many years later, in early 2003 to be exact, a friend of mine was giving an intimate cocktail party for a few close friends and called me up with a unique invitation. "I have an old friend of yours standing here," he said. "From your past. He'd love to see you …"

The hosts were long-time friends and I had nothing better going on, so I eagerly accepted and, upon arrival, was warmly greeted by all those in attendance. Including an instantly recognizable IBM big wig from my World's Fair days. We're talking about forty years ago.

"Jed, you old so and so," he said after a quick but pleasant re-introduction. "Do you remember me? I'm the guy who hired you to work the IBM Pavillion at the 64–65 World's Fair in Flushing Meadows …"

"Sure, I remember," I said calmly over the mutual tinkling of our freshly filled rocks glasses. "You're the guy who fired me, too."

Blushing, the former IBM exec quickly went into damage control. "Oh, gee," he fumbled, "I hope there's no hard feelings …"

"That's okay," I grinned. "I forgot all about it … just last week!"

Love of Life

Back in 1951, one of television's first live serials debuted and, in daytime, *stayed* live until 1967. Set in the fictional town of Rosehill, New York, *Love of Life* was a popular daytime drama that over the decades garnered a wide and loyal following who, amazingly, kept it on the air until its final episode sometime in 1980.

Created by behind-the-scenes television legend Roy Windsor, who would later enter my life on my second soap opera, *Love of Life* asked me to join their cast shortly after I was summarily dismissed from the IBM Pavilion.

I was to play a despicable character, the bad guy, the heavy, the heavy, heavy bad guy named Ace Hubbard, truly one of the classic soap opera names of all time. Among his many dubious achievements, Ace once had the pleasure of knocking around a pregnant woman in front of millions of loyal viewers.

Truly, this was a stretch for me because as Don Rickel's theme song says, "I'm a nice guy …"

There's a wonderful story about working on live television that sums up perfectly what I was feeling shortly after joining the cast of *Love of Life* in the mid-60s. Eva Marie Saint was working on the live television drama *I Remember Mama* with her co-star, Philip Dorn, who played "Papa."

Now Dorn had been a matinee idol back in Germany and Holland, before fleeing his homeland in the early days of World War II to reinvent himself in Hollywood. Apparently he'd played one too many roles because, by the time he wound up on the set with Eva-Marie in the 1950s, he was having a hard time remembering his lines.

Live TV is a harsh and unforgiving mistress, and flubbed lines are the bane of an actor's existence once he signs the dotted line on his player's contract. Missed, out of sequence, or even forgotten lines can lead to the ruination of a scene or, occasionally, the stuff of which legends are made of.

Such was the case when "Papa" sat next to Eva Marie Saint on the set of *I Remember Mama* one memorable evening. The scene was taking place on an airplane, flying thousands of feet in the air as Eva and Papa muddled through another tense scene where Dorn occasionally flubbed his lines. At one point, he forgot them entirely, leaving poor Eva sitting there in mid-air with only one recourse: A quick ad-lib.

"This," quipped the frustrated actress, "is where I get off …"

As for myself, maybe I should have "gotten off" before even getting on.

So many stories, so little time …

Ace Gets Axed

The pressures of live TV are as exhilarating as they are excruciating, and working on my first live TV set, not to mention daytime serial or, as they were to later be termed, "soap opera," was a heady experience for a twenty-something actor on the rise.

Jed Allan

I Remembered Mama all too well and thus memorized my lines eagerly and voraciously with every script change, bound and determined not to let my first television role slip through my hands.

Or off of my tongue …

I worked with many fine actors during my stint on the live daytime serial, one of whom was only sixteen at the time. Bonnie Bedelia, who played the role of Sandy Porter from 1961 to 1967, was a good-hearted, fresh faced teenager when I worked with her on *Love of Life*.

But that didn't stop her from bringing home the bacon …

Now widely recognized as the star of two *Die Hard* films with Bruce Willis and the calculating wife of Harrison Ford in *Presumed Innocent*, among other fine roles that continue to display her fine acting abilities, Bonnie was supporting her entire family on her soap wages and, even then, her quiet dignity made an impression on me that floods back whenever I see her in feature films or on TV.

Despite the fact that my character, Ace Hubbard, was as despicable as they come, I tried my best to make him a likable anti-hero, all to no avail. Still, I was riding this ratings train for all it was worth and my only regret was that I never actually got to see myself perform!

This was long before VCRs or videotapes, and something like Tivo might as well have been a lunar landing craft as far as broadcast television was concerned in the mid-60s. My only barometer as to each day's performance was when I would race home to Toby after a long day on the set and asked her, "How was I today, honey?"

Fortunately, she rarely had any complaints …

Unfortunately, other viewers did. After four months on the set of *Love of Life*, my character Ace Hubbard was written out of any and all future scripts. Today it's cliché to have your character "written out," but in those days it was often traumatic and, personally, I felt a stabbing twinge of failure.

I'd tried in vain to make Ace "likable," but there's only so much you can do with a poorly written, poorly conceived, black, black, *black* character … no matter how cool his name was. I left the set of *Love of Life* with four months' worth of experience—and a brand new Rolodex full of fresh, high-powered industry contacts.

Shortly, one in particular would pay off with my *second* soap role …

Sadly, *Love of Life* would go on without me. But in inevitable Hollywood fashion, the soap opera would live on for nearly two more decades and spawn at least one "six degrees of separation" relationship that would soon make this TV newbie feel like an industry veteran: The "child actor" who played Jamie Rawlins Number Two on the show from1970 to 1976 was a fresh faced young rookie named Ian Ziering.

In the mid-90s, I would go on to play Ian's father on *Beverly Hills 90210*…

"My Teeth Feel Soft …"

An incredible thing happened while on the way to appearing in my second live soap: The Broadway smash *Barefoot in the Park*. The brilliant script by Neil Simon, directed by Mike Nichols, had opened at the famed Biltmore Theatre on West 47th Street on October 23, 1963.

Two years later it was still going stronger than ever …

Its original cast boasted such heavyweights as Elizabeth Ashley as newlywed Corie Bratter, Kurt Kasznar as her lothario neighbor Victor Velasco, Mildred Natwick as the mother-in-law, Mrs. Banks, and a young Robert Redford playing hapless newlywed turned loving husband Paul Bratter.

Since Redford, both Robert Reed and Tony Roberts had stepped into Paul Bratter's shoes on Broadway. Soon, I was about to try them on for size as well. Not as an understudy, which had helped me land the sometime roll of Bill Sykes in *Oliver!*, but this time I was to be hired as something known as a "standby."

Though the name might not *sound* particularly impressive, the perks certainly were. Understudies must hang around, night and day, forever waiting for that call that so and so is drunk, such and such broke two fingers, or whatnot. But as a standby, all I had to do was call into the theater half an hour before the show and "check in." If all was going according to plan and either Tony Roberts or Robert Reed were already in makeup, I was free to go about my business and rest assured that the evening's performance would go off without a hitch.

The schedule worked great for me, particularly considering I was still starring on *The Hidden Hurricane* at the time. I played Paul Bratter on Broadway many times as a standby during the 1965–1966 season, and every Wednesday during the matinee.

This being the era of live television, my matinee status provided the producers of my popular soap opera with a challenging dilemma: What to do without a lead character every Wednesday? Thankfully, they were kind enough to write me out each Wednesday so that I was free should they need me on standby.

Then again, looking back, how hard can it be to switch things around on daytime TV? After all, look at how many people have died off, and then been brought back from the dead, on some of today's favorite soaps?

Both the role, and the play, were true highlights in my career and I consider myself fortunate to be a part of the formidable *Barefoot in the Park* legacy. The play, which still tours the country annually in dinner theaters from Pittsburgh to Poughkeepsie, has been done by many lead actors over the years and, whenever I can, I make it a habit to stop in and check out the competition.

While I've certainly seen some actors do better in the lead roles than others, I have to say that I've never seen anyone do it badly. I have to give credit to the playwright for this, however. The play is written so perfectly, the timing of each line choreographed so well, that it's almost impossible to screw up.

I, of course, thought I was the best …

My favorite moment of doing the play each night was the scene in which, as Paul Bratter, I would carry my drunken mother-in-law, Mrs. Banks, up four flights of stairs to flop her down on the living room couch, both of us facing the audience.

I used to love to listen to the audience howl and, as we sat there on the couch waiting for the laughter to die so we could deliver our next lines, I used to count off the seconds to see how long I could keep the audience laughing without doing anything, physically, other than staring at them as I tried to catch my breath.

Believe it or not, every performance was different. Some nights the laughter lasted much longer than other nights. It all depended on the type of audience. Or, very often, the actor. I got to the point where I could cut it off whenever I wanted to. That was the essence of comedy: Learning the knack of when to turn it off, when to turn it on.

Sometimes forever is too short …

My first line after hauling her up all that way and sitting there, trying to catch my breath after walking up those several dozen stairs and downing just as many shots of high-octane Uzo throughout the evening is the showstopper, "My teeth feel … soft."

And the next line, "I can't make a fist." Equally perfect lines.

Those were precious moments indeed …

I wish I could say the same for my one chance meeting with the playwright. Many years later, walking out of a popular Hamburger Hamlet chain in California, I instantly recognized the bespectacled author on his way in. Eager to capitalize on my chance to thank the author of what I consider to be one of the finer plays in theater, I cleared my throat and said, "Excuse me, Mr. Simon. I'm Jed Allan. I don't think you remember me, but I did your show, *Barefoot in the Park*, on Broadway in 1965 and '66."

Expecting a handshake, or at least a polite brush-off, I got neither. Instead, the man of so many words muttered, "That's nice" and walked inside to get his burger. I guess he used up his best lines in all those great plays.

Galoshes in the Park?

1966 was dead and gone, and with it two of my biggest roles to date. I was now happily married eight years, Toby was a glowing mother of not one, not two, but *three* healthy boys, and together we had a trio to watch over, care for, and protect.

As I was walking down Broadway late that same year, short on cash and once again considering a return to my recurring role in Taxi Cab Confessions, Take 3, I happened to glance up and realize I was standing in front of the old Winter Garden Theater, where I'd done *All-American* with Ray Bolger.

Fondly remembering my past triumphs and wondering when, or even *if*, I'd have another, I was tapped on the shoulder by one of my favorite people in the whole world. "Jed?" asked a familiar voice and, when I turned around, there stood the general manager of Bucks County Playhouse, Mike Ellis. "How are you?"

We hugged and shared a few glory days before catching up on those currently at hand. After hearing of my latest accomplishments, Mike looked me up and down and admitted, "You're not going to believe this, but I'm doing a reading tomorrow and, believe it or not, you'd be dead on for the role. Are you interested?"

Was I interested? Here I was considering another starring role behind the steering wheel of a checkered cab and along comes the offer for another Broadway part. "You have a contract with you?" I asked in jest. "Of course I'm interested, just tell me where and when."

After telling me a little about the play, called the *Paisley Convertible*, Mike told me to show up for a reading at his office by 2:00 o'clock the next day. Not quite an audition, a reading for a play is generally attended only by the playwright, in this case Harry Cauley, the producer himself, and the actors he already has in mind for the parts. I quickly learned that the ensemble piece would have a slight resemblance to *Barefoot in the Park*.

After we all got acquainted, the reading was held precisely at two-thirty the next day and attended by five actors Mike felt were "good for the part," as nothing was cast in stone, including me, I thought, among them Joyce Bulifant, a lovely and talented actress who would later go on to play Mrs. Davis in the 1980 cult classic, *Airplane!*

Her husband was no slouch, either. James McArthur, later to become the star of *Hawaii 5–0*, not to mention my current neighbor, literally came from Broadway royalty. The son of one of the great leading ladies of all time, Helen Hayes, and the author of *Front Page*, playwright Charles McArthur, James' pedigree was almost as impressive as his taste in women. All three of them.

I loved the reading. I loved the play. I even loved the part I'd read for, Ralph Keppelman. Sounds like a nerd and, come to think of it, he was a nerd. Several days later I got the call. After being awarded the part, I told Mike, "That's great. Thanks so much. Hey, listen, who else made it?"

"Only you and Joyce," Mike answered, surprising me since I thought the others were very talented actors. "But don't feel too bad, we've got a great cast: Sam Waterston, Marsha Hunt, and Betsy Von Fustenberg."

Great cast, indeed …

Unlike many of my previous Broadway experiences, the *Paisley Convertible* wouldn't be "going on the road" at all. We faced five weeks of rehearsals, two weeks of previews with a live audience, and then opening night, all right there on 43rd Street.

From the very beginning, my fellow cast members impressed me. I was already familiar with Joyce's great work, and her fellow female players were equally impressive. Betsy Von Furstenberg was a top-notch performer with a top-notch background. She'd already done considerable work on Broadway, including *Much Ado About Nothing, Nature's Way, Child of Fortune,* and *The Chalk Garden,* but despite her storied family history and moneyed last name, in the end, she was just another of us.

I'll never forget the time Betsy and I were trading industry gossip and talking about who we admired, and detested, on stage and screen. For some reason, Betsy had a real thing for Tony Randall. And not in a good way, either.

"I can't stand him," she told me one day during rehearsals.

"Why?" I asked, surprised. "He's terrific."

"Maybe," she'd sneered. "But what a pain in the ass! He's so picky about everything. One time I was so pissed at him that, during our kissing scene in *Oh Men! Oh Women!* I shoved a clam down his throat, just to knock him off his high horse. It was only funny to me, I guess, watching him choke. He certainly didn't think so …"

"What did he do?" I asked, shocked.

"Reported me to Equity," she stated flatly, obviously unscathed from the incident. "So, in retaliation, the next time we did a scene together I put Alum in his drink. Boy, you should have seen that tight ass pucker!"

Naturally, the measly fine she got from the powers that be at Equity for this second offense barely made a dent in the family fortune …

90

Jed Allan

Marsha Hunt had been a former Powers model until she made her onscreen debut in 1935's *The Virginia Judge* at only eighteen years of age. Since then her numerous onscreen and stage appearances had made her an actress of note by the time I finally met her on the *Paisley Convertible*. Years later, upon running into Ms. Hunt at some function or another, I asked her if she remembered me from our time onstage together.

"Why yes," she said after close scrutiny. "You're that guy who taught me how to sing 'If I Were a Rich Man!'"

Such was the legacy of her first Jewish co-star …

Naturally, the other male lead, Sam Waterston, was particularly strong, both onstage and off. Even back then there was definitely a presence about the man, and I felt he would go far. Unfortunately, I wasn't so sure comedy was his … *forte*.

Apparently our director, James Hammerstein, Jr., son of famed writer and producer Oscar Hammerstein, agreed. Less than four weeks into rehearsals, the producers fired Sam Waterston from the *Paisley Convertible*. Meanwhile, Mike Ellis had already left for California to find a replacement for Sam.

Said Sam of the event years later, "Getting fired from *Paisley Convertible* was a terribly valuable experience." Maybe so, but I don't think he felt so at the time. The way I remember it, Sam was so upset he showed up for rehearsals. Drunk. And it showed. Sadly, his antics that day earned him his only laughs to date.

I couldn't blame the guy. After all, comedy isn't for everybody. Likewise, however, playing comedy isn't any big secret. You just can't be afraid to act silly. You have to have a sense of humor, not just about life, but about yourself. If you can't act silly, can't laugh at yourself, you just can't do comedy. Definitely not a hard and fast rule, just a guideline for being funny.

Sam wasn't very funny in the play and, frankly, I doubt he's very funny today …

Sam might not have been a comedian, but he had an eye for the truth. All actors should remember another quote from Sam, cause it's really true: "You can't get into the 'I know best, I won't be told' thing, but you have to take full responsibility for what you accept from the director—and then instruct him in what his decision means. You can't just say, 'I'm doing the director's concept and see how good or how bad it is.'"

All true, Sam. And you certainly practice what you preach. You've got a hell of a career. And after all this time, you probably don't even remember me …

That replacement Mike had flown to California to sign? Upon his arrival back on the East coast we learned that it was none other than Bill Bixby. "Jed," said Mike just after he'd introduced us all to Bill, "you've got your work cut out for you. You've got less than ten days to help get Bill ready for this show."

I said it then and I'll say it now, "It would be my privilege …"

Where Sam was a serious actor who found it hard to be silly, Bill was a serious actor who was also very funny. Funny as a friend. Funny as an actor. He'd already been on Broadway in *Under the Yum Yum Tree*, and his future roles, including those in such beloved television favorites as *My Favorite Martian*, *The Courtship of Eddie's Father*, and, of course, *The Incredible Hulk*, revealed his wide range of acting styles.

A scholar and a gentleman, later years would find him on the other side of the camera. At the time of his untimely death from prostate cancer, Bill Bixby was principal director of the TV series *Blossom*. For now, however, he was merely my colleague and, true to form, he got up to speed for a very demanding role in less than ten days. Still, humble as ever, he would give me credit for as long as I knew him. Years later, whenever we showed up at this function or on a set, Bill would always introduce me with warmth, enthusiasm, and class.

"I want you to meet a guy who really saved my ass," he'd say, be it to a crowd of one or one hundred. "I had ten days to learn a part on Broadway and this guy really pulled me through it. Folks … Jed Allan."

Unfortunately, the critics weren't so kind. Despite the revamped cast, Bixby's enthusiasm, and our unwavering loyalty to the material and its director, the *Paisley Convertible* ran for just nine performances, from February 11, 1967 to the 18th.

The reviews, admittedly, were mixed. But I could hardly complain. Said one prominent New York newspaper, "If we get nothing else out of *The Paisley Convertible*, we've got a new Fred MacMurray in Jed Allan." High praise indeed.

But while that line has stuck with me for lo these last four decades, another piece of slick newspaper copy apparently doomed the play from the very beginning. Said the same reviewer, "The Paisley Convertible is another version of Breakfast in the Park. Let's call it 'Galoshes in the Park'…"

The most memorable moment for me about "Galoshes" was the party at Sardi's restaurant after the opening. I walked in and actually got a standing ovation. Toby cried, and I almost fainted. Such a joy. And then the reviews come out.

The play died.

Once again, I was out of work …

My final tribute came a day later from the great actress Helen Hayes, Joyce's mother-in-law. It was a telegram that said, "Dear Jed, You're a joy." It's laminated and has been hanging up in my den since 1967.

Escape From New York

I'd been out of work for a month by the time Toby and I agreed to leave New York and head out to California, but it took three more weeks for us to pack and finally get out of dodge. It's common for actors, producers, directors, and other industry types to leap frog from one coast to the other, and occasionally back again, but it was a first for Toby and I and, with close family ties to New York, not a very easy one at that.

But it was getting to be the late 60s by now and the writing was clearly on the wall. The living room wall, that is: Television was the wave of the future. Broadway plays were growing few and far between while it seemed television series were popping up all over the place. It didn't take a rocket scientist, let alone an ex-cab driver, to see that an actor could find more work on television than on stage.

Despite my firm allegiance to the stage, with five Broadway plays under my belt by this point, the future—California was calling me and, I hoped better things in store.

Please, Spell the Name Right

My sister, who had already moved to California, helped us find a house in sunny Woodland Hills for only $230 a month. It was an opportunity I couldn't pass up, and after a tearful goodbye to family and friends, Toby and I found ourselves stranded on the tarmac at LaGuardia Airport on April 6, 1967.

For two hours our three precious boys, Mitch, who was six, Dean, who was three, and Rick, who was barely a year old by this point, sat quietly in their seats. The perfect little angels. But the minute the plane took off, two-thirds of our formerly peaceful brood started wailing—and didn't let up until we landed at LAX several hours later.

There was no valium in those days, either.

Welcome to sunny California …

Make it 10%

Many actors come to the West coast penniless, or so say their dubious publicity bios once they've made it big. As for myself, I landed in sunny California with $5,000 in my pocket.

And I earned every cent of it.

Or, to be more precise, soon would …

There was no way Toby and I could have made the move to Woodland Hills, and our new three-bedroom home, without a little help. My father didn't have that kind of dough, bless his heart, but my mother's uncles, Alex and Irving Ross, certainly did.

Hat in hand, I asked them for the five grand. But knowing the type of men they were, make that *businessmen*, I made them a proposition first: "You loan me five grand now, and I'll pay you five percent of what I make for the next ten years."

Without batting an eye their decision was unanimous. "Make it ten percent," they said, "and you've got a deal."

And thus I arrived in California with a bankroll, but my uncles certainly got their investment back, in spades. Over the next six and a half years I would pay them close to $18,000 as part of our "gentlemen's agreement."

But they were just one of many hangers on with their hand out. At the time I had an agent, and soon a manger, both naturally getting ten percent of what I made. All part of the business, I understood, but paying my uncles was getting harder.

And so, on a brief vacation nearly seven years into my business agreement with my uncles, I said to Toby, "Damn, I forgot to send Alex and Irving their check this month."

Toby turned to me and said, "I really feel, honey, that they've gotten enough from us for their five grand." And I really, in my heart, felt the same way.

Once again, she was right. I didn't pay. Weeks later I got a call from my uncles complaining about the sudden—and apparently unexpected—lapse in payment. "What?" they asked. "You go on vacation and forgot to pay us?"

"Forgot to pay you?" I said. "I've shelled out over eighteen grand in just over six years. That should be plenty. How can you ask for more?"

What's the old saying? Never do business with family or friends? I learned that the hard way. For years there was bad blood between my uncles and me, blood that spilled over into the opinions of their sons and daughters, my cousins.

While we can finally joke about it today, it's only been in the last ten years or so that we've actually begun *laughing* about it. It still gets a chuckle from all of us, though I'm sure Irving and Alex are rolling over in their graves.

Big Break, Big Valley

I'd gotten my new West coast agent, Bill Barnes, through a New York friend and it proved to be a wise choice when he quickly hit pay dirt with my very first audition. It was for the hit TV series, *The Big Valley*, and I got the part right out of the gate. Set in the 1870's in California's gorgeous San Joaquin Valley, *The Big Valley* is the story of Stockton's richest and most powerful family the Barkleys.

I'd long been a fan of the series and working on set with some of its stars, particularly the legendary Barbra Stanwyck, was heady stuff for a boy from the Bronx. Still, I held my own in Episode Number 64, "The Time after Midnight," which first aired on October 2, 1967.

But more so than the one episode I guest starred on, *Big Valley* was equally important for the ego boost it gave me during my first few months in California. "Shit," I remember thinking, "this is gonna be easy."

My next roll, on the big screen no less, only made it seem even easier …

Remember the Name: *Your Life May Depend on It …*
Based on the novel by Alistair MacLean and directed by John Sturges, *Ice Station Zebra* was an action vehicle for its two A-List stars, Rock Hudson and Ernest Borgnine. The tagline for the film and in the 60s, perhaps more so than today, they *all* had taglines, was: "Ice Station Zebra. Remember The Name—Your Life May Depend On It!"

At the time, it certainly felt like mine did …

I was thrilled to get the part in *Ice Station Zebra*, playing the role of Costigan, a fathometer operator on a sub. Well, that's pretty stupid. Where else would a fathometer operator be but on a sub? I was "the great and grand measurer of ice." Or so I gathered after reading a script in which I had nearly sixty-five lines, each of them some variation of the words, "Thin ice. Thin ice. Thin ice …"

As for the variations? Well, there was the occasional addition of an actual ice *measurement* to my standard lines. As in the riveting, "Thin ice. Twelve feet. Thin ice. Thin ice …" Or the equally memorable, "Thin ice. Thin ice. Six feet. Thin ice …"

Hardly Shakespeare, but nonetheless eighteen weeks of the most fun I've had in the business up until then. The storyline was a familiar one for action flicks in the late 60s: "Commander James Ferraday (Hudson), USN, has new orders: Get David Jones, a British civilian, Captain Anders, a tough Marine with a platoon of troops, Boris Vasilov (Borgnine), a friendly Russian, and the crew of the nuclear sub USS Tigerfish to the North Pole to rescue the crew of Drift Ice Station Zebra, a weather station at the top of the world. The mission takes on new and dangerous twists as the crew finds out that all is not as it seems at Zebra, and that someone will stop at nothing to prevent the mission from being completed..."

Think *Guns of Navarone* meets *North to Alaska* and you'll have an idea of what it was like traipsing around the 100-degree-plus back lot at MGM studios in parkas, ski pants, and snow boots for eighteen long, hot weeks.

The boys and I—Rock, Ron Masak, Bill Hillman, and Lloyd Haines—played a lot of Hearts in Rock's trailer, and I can honestly say that those moments of camaraderie, a star and his legions, and cards are forever frozen in my mind as some of the finest in my life.

And despite being pigeonholed as a "60s action flick," the actors with whom I worked never gave anything less than their best, behind the scenes or in front of the camera. I can vividly remember Ernie Borgnine coming in on his days off to stand opposite Rock for Rock's close-ups, even though generally a script supervisor would usually do it if the actor wasn't around for some reason. But there was Ernie, reading his lines with affect and aplomb, all so old Rock could get the most out of his lines. Very unusual.

Pros to the end, that's how I'll fondly remember both men ...

Ernie, still being alive, I see once in awhile. Rock was something special. But Rock and Ernie weren't the only stars I'll remember from that eighteen-week shoot. Football legend Jim Brown played Captain Leslie Anders, of the United States Marine Corps, while Ron Masek played Chief Petty Officer Paul Zabrinczski. Ron and I formed a close bond that lasts to this day. After thirty years of buying season tickets to the Dodgers together, it better.

Bill Hillman, another "Ice actor," had bigger plans in store. Years later, as both writer and director, Hillman would later use me in a 1975 film, *The Man from Clover Grove*, playing a young hippy. Or, as it is listed in the actual credits, "*The* Hippy."

Better to be a "the" than an "a" any day, I suppose ...

But Bill and Ron weren't the only hangovers from *Ice Station Zebra* to keep popping up in my life. Lee Stanly, another actor from the 60s flick, would later go on to direct me in a Christian boxing movie for the Trinity Broadcasting Network called *Carmen, the Champion.*

The actor playing Webson, Lloyd Haynes, got his start working behind the camera as a television crewman, though after *Ice Station Zebra* he would eventually go on to land a leading role in the television series *Room 222.*

Luckily, Lloyd was as good a sport as he was an actor for, as the sole

African-American in our endless card games in Rock's trailer, he was often the brunt of several merciless, if hilarious, practical jokes.

Case in point: One day, instead of eating at the commissary as per usual, we had a hankering for McDonald's but had to leave the studio lot to do so. Lloyd graciously volunteered, perhaps less out of goodwill and more out of the chance to drive Rock's prized Corvette around the mean streets of Culver City.

Seizing this priceless opportunity, we immediately called the security gate and alerted the guard that "Rock Hudson's car has been stolen and, gasp, a … black man … was seen at the wheel …" In minutes poor Lloyd was stopped at the gate and brought straight to Mr. Hudson.

In handcuffs, no less …

It was hard to keep a straight face as Rock "identified" the "assailant," particularly with Lloyd whining, "Come on guys, this isn't funny anymore." Despite our combined resumes, we weren't such great actors that we could continue fooling the hapless security guard for too long, though to his credit he played his part well.

Eventually, however, Lloyd was "released into our custody" and spent the rest of the shoot trying to repay us in kind. Luckily, he was not suited to the role of practical joker and never succeeded.

We never did get our Big Macs that day …

The Dog is the Star

All good things must come to an end, and such was the case when *Ice Station Zebra* finally wrapped in October of 1967. I bid goodbye to big stars and good friends, not to mention sixty-five particularly "icy" lines, and was able to spend some quality time with Toby and the boys in our house in Woodland Hills.

Months went by, 1967 eventually crawled into 1968, and before I knew it an entire year had passed! Just as I was beginning to sweat ever getting another role in Hollywood again, my agent called offering me a guest role on television's favorite kids' show, *Lassie*.

Airing at seven p.m. on Sunday nights, the dog show with a heart certainly had legs, and had been on television since the mid-1950s. I was thrilled to be offered the role, actually *any* role by that point, and didn't even complain when I had to travel to puny Cape Canaveral, Florida to complete the gig.

Meeting the show's stars was a treat, particularly Robert Bray, who played Park Ranger Corey Stuart from 1964 to 1969, and though "the Cape," as it was known, was just a little air force base town at the time, there were other perks as well.

In the late 1960s the Apollo-Saturn missions were in full swing off the Cape, and one fine October night in 1968 I witnessed the majestic launch of a Saturn rocket off of Florida's burgeoning Space Coast.

Unfortunately, Lassie himself left less of an impression …

Biting the Hand That Feeds You?

Two months after my guest shot on Episode 461 of *Lassie*, "The Bracelet," appeared, the producers of Lassie once again called me out of the blue. "Would you," they asked, "be interested in playing one of the new Forest Rangers for the new season coming up?"

"Sure," I answered. "But what happened to the *old* Forest Ranger?"

Apparently the "old Forest Ranger," Robert Bray, had a minor drinking problem, okay, *major* drinking problem and, one tragic night, while talking to one of his no less than seven ex-wives on the phone in his trailer he'd become so distraught that he'd literally shot off his own hand.

The 60s were getting more and more progressive, but one-handed Forest Rangers were still a little too much. Especially on Sunday nights at 7:00. Why, what would the kiddies think?

And so, yours truly was up for his first starring role on an evening drama. Weekly evening drama. Evening weekly drama for kids.

Starring a dog …

But first, I had to jump through a few hoops of my own. An initial meeting with the show's producers, Robert Golden and Bill Beaudine, went particularly well, though it ended with the same non-committal words I would hear so often over the next few months, not to mention my entire career, "We'll let you know."

A couple weeks later I got a call that "I was getting closer" but that I would need to meet with the show's two *other* producer-owners, Jack Wrather and Bonita Granville. Once again, I had a great meeting that ended with, "Well, it's been a pleasure. It looks very good. We'll let you know."

Another few weeks go by, I get another phone call, this time from the studio's secretary. "Mr. Allan, everybody is very pleased with you so far. There's just one more person you need to meet."

"Who?" I asked, expecting to hear the name of yet another producer, director, or, perhaps, studio big wig.

But the secretary seemed taken aback that I would even ask such a question. "Why, Lassie, of course," she stammered.

Before I could stop myself, I said, "You gotta be kidding me."

Dead silence. Eventually, the very devoted secretary explained patiently, "Mr. Allan. If the dog does not like you, how can you possibly play against him?"

"Very valid point," I had to admit, since I wasn't a real animal person.

Marveling to my endlessly devoted wife about the "dog and pony" show I was being forced to put on for this Sunday night's kid show, Toby had another great idea. "You know," she said with a glimmer in those beautiful eyes that I just knew I was going to regret, "Our friends, George and Adele, have a dog and, well, it's in heat at the moment."

"Bravo," I said. "What does that have to do with me?"

"Well," said Toby patiently, ever the teacher. "They live in Van Nuys, which is on the way to the studio. On the day of your meeting, you should go over, roll around with their dog, and get her scent all over you. That way, old Lassie won't be able to resist you."

Genius. Pure genius. Toby knew, as did I, that Lassie was, in fact, a male. Not because boy dogs act better than girl dogs—though I suspect all males are better at taking direction, from women anyway—but because female Collies molt in the summer and would thus interrupt regular year-round shooting schedules.

And so, on the appointed day or, perhaps, one might say "anointed day," I stopped by our friend George and Adele's house. As always, I was dressed to the nines and although rolling around with a dog before an interview was anathema to yours truly, I did as I was told and carefully draped my expensive blazer over our friends' randy bitch.

While my coat was soaking up her aromatic musk, I got on the ground and played around until I felt I was sufficiently covered in "dog perfume." Then it was back out to Culver City Studios to meet with none other than Lassie herself, er, himself.

You might not know the name, but you'd certainly recognize the studio's front office which might be better known to all you Margaret Mitchell fans as the exterior for Scarlet O'Hara's family estate, Tara.

Unfortunately, after another hour with the show's producers answering the same old questions and waiting for the dog of the hour to arrive, I finally got up the nerve to ask, "When do I meet Lassie?"

"Oh," they assured me, "in about an hour. And it's a half-hour drive to Saugus, where we keep Lassie."

"Shit," I thought, covertly sniffing myself. I'd been over an hour with the producers, had another hour to go, and then a half hour drive. That's nearly three hours for the dog perfume to wash off.

Luckily, I was given directions to Saugus, which was off the 405 Freeway and just happened to be north of Van Nuys. And so, once my final interview with the producers was up I hopped in the car, went straight back to George and Adele's backyard for another quick shot of doggy perfume, and then straight to Saugus.

Freshly dowsed in female pooch hormones, I arrived at Lassie's home away from home and was pleasantly surprised when the star dog leapt from his kennel as soon as it was opened and licked me as if we'd been friends for over a decade. (That's seventy seasons in dog years.)

Needless to say, I got the part.

I always wondered what my sidekick that season, Jack De Mave, did to get hired …

"What Do You Say, Lassie?"

I was paid $750 per episode for Lassie, later to be bumped to $800 and, finally, $1,100, and did fifteen episodes a season for two seasons. Not exactly prime rib, but nor was it dog food, either. Being on TV's top rated Sunday night drama wasn't so bad after all.

Even when the producers told me, literally, these were the words they used, "The dog's the star …"

He was, too. I wasn't allowed to do any publicity without Lassie and, frankly, we were all but inseparable during those two long years. Even when we traveled. By law, in my contract, literally, there was a "travel clause," Lassie was required to travel first class with me everywhere we went. To this day, Lassie is still the only animal ever allowed to fly first class on a commercial airliner. True, he was in a box, but he was in a box sitting in first class.

And travel we did. I got to see much of the country I otherwise wouldn't have as a result of the producers' wish to transport Lassie, and thus the series, to exotic destinations in an effort to boost ratings and add depth to an otherwise two-dimensional character.

Thanks to Lassie, I've been salmon fishing in glacial lakes in Alaska and all over the world. There were other perks, too, such as the time I "co-starred" with a live wolf. Though the producers were going to use a stunt double to place "my" hands inside the wild animal's jaws during a particularly tense scene, I realized the animal had been sedated and offered to do it myself.

After all, I figured, it would look better for the audience if they actually saw "me" saving the wild beast, as opposed to a pair of "stunt hands" standing in. Reluctantly, I was allowed to do so even though, when the episode later aired, all the cameraman shot was my hands anyway.

Still, you couldn't say I wasn't trying …

There were other challenges to working with animals as well. For instance, when working with humans, timing is less of an issue. We are all programmed to say our lines once the other actor has delivered theirs.

"*Thank* you."

"Your *welcome.*"

"Hello."

"*Hello.*"

"Goodbye."

"Goodbye ...."

Boom. Bam. Just like that. But with a dog, or any other animal actor for that matter, there is an interminable wait until you can "play off of him." For instance, when Lassie would "speak," a favorite of his childhood audience, it took a guy sitting over my shoulder on a ladder making "doggie signs" to finally get him to do so.

So instead of a quick back-and-forth between actors, a scene with Lassie usually went thusly:

"What do you say, Lassie?" says the dedicated actor into the camera.

Next, the guy over my shoulder does his thing, which I never actually got to see for myself because he was always behind my back, while the camera rolls in Lassie's face.

Suddenly, or not so suddenly, in most cases, but always out of nowhere, "Bark. Bark."

"I agree," says the dedicated actor with a sigh. "Let's go get some hamburger meat ..."

It was just like working with Everett Horton all over again ...

My kids, on the other hand, were thrilled their "daddy" was working with America's favorite pooch, and were never happier than when visiting their old man on the set. One day, however, I made the mistake of letting them feed Lassie and his owner-trainer, Rudd Weatherwax, went ballistic.

"Who are these children?" he bellowed, scaring my three boys to near tears. "What are they doing feeding my dog? Who told them they could do that? No one feeds my dog on my set, etc."

I explained to Rudd what had happened and, though he never apologized, I never let the kids feed Lassie again. Such was the price of doggy fame ...

Three year old Jed

I was cute at age ten...

"All American"
Eileen Hurley, Ray Bolger and me playing the devil

Bill Bixby and me in a scene from
"The Paisley Convertable" on Broadway

Milton Berle and me in "Guys and Dolls"
at the Dorothy Chandler Pavillion

Ranger "Scott Turner" and Lassie, 1970

Jack DeMave is the other guy

"Ice Station Zebra"
From left to Right: John Sturges, Jed Allan, Michael Greenblat,
Rock Hudson

"Celebrity Bowling Show"
From left to right: Bobby Troup, Bob Newhart, Jed Allan,
Robert Culp, Roy Rogers

Game Show "Bounce Back" with me as the host, our contestant,
and actor Robert Pine

"Brenda Starr" with Jill St. John

Interview in Tallinn, Estonia with Louise Sorel and me

Toby and her husband

In the "Hee Haw" cornfield with George Lindsey, formerly
"Goober" in "Mayberry RFD"

Leslie Nielson and me

Scene from "Santa Barbara" with the band Air Supply
and Robin Mattson

Judith McConnell and me looking younger for a flashback scene on
"Santa Barbara"

Toby with my boys, Mitch, Rick and Dean

The 70s:
"He's Not Nighttime, He's Daytime …"

Looking back, I can honestly say that the 1970s were a beautifully, deliciously, busily, wonderfully sweet time of my young life. It seemed I was involved in so many things: Guest appearances on the decade's hottest TV shows, my own theater, guest hosting gigs on talk shows, you name it. I was really loving this time of my professional life.

And as for my family life? It couldn't have been better. Well, that's not entirely true, either. The kids, in fact, could have been better. A *lot* better! My three boys—Mitch, Dean, and Rick—were growing up beautifully, if … difficultly.

Toby was her usually, bubbly, beautiful self, but so busy with the three guys at that time I honestly don't know how she managed to pull it off. But pull it off she did. They were so fun, and yet so tough, to be with. Sometimes, honestly, it was murder to be around them. They played like boys, they fought like boys—they ate in restaurants like boys. In other words, we didn't eat out a lot.

We also needed a maid …

Toby and I used to fantasize about getting a nanny, counting our pennies and dreaming of the day when we could hand our three little hellions, er, boys, over to somebody *else* for a change. We used to beg our friends not to invite our kids to anything they invited *us* to come to—or we simply couldn't come.

They were typically boys, but they were tough to bring up. They were, and are, beautiful, sensitive, intelligent, loving, giving young men. Toby did a great job. However, in those days, they could test the patience of Job himself. In fact, we had some friends who were childless who would come over just to validate the fact that not having kids themselves was okay.

That's how bad they were …

But getting on with my career, it was moving swiftly along. I was happy with the strides I was making. The 70s brought me success in many areas. Little did I imagine the first of them would be with a bowling ball in my hand.

Long Weekends …

Not long after the 60s had faded away and the 70s were upon us, my press agent at the time, Joe Siegman, decided to dip his foot in the deep end of television production and, along with his partner Don Gregory, thought the stale talk show format needed a swift kick in the pants.

The result of their brainstorm? *Celebrity Bowling.*

Their choice for a host? Yours truly …

Part *Merv Griffin*, part *Wide World of Sports*, part *Kingpin*, the idea behind *Celebrity Bowling* was simple: "Four celebrities, on two teams of two, competed in a standard ten-frame game of bowling. Each team was playing for members of the studio audience. The team with the highest score won the day's top prize for their designated studio audience member."

What could I say? The gig was good, the money was better.

Much better …

The best part about it was I only worked three days a week. Specifically, long weekends. Little did I know how long they would actually be. To save money, not to mention time, the producers got the bright idea to shoot only on long weekends. That meant we shot ten half-hour shows in a single day. Ten costume changes in a day. Forty celebrity interviews in a day. No scripts, and thirty shows wrapped, cut, and "in the can" by Monday afternoon.

It was a dizzying schedule, particularly with my duties on *Lassie* still winding down, but the chance to host a celebrity talk show and watch screen legends old and new sail a bowling ball down a custom designed lane toward ten quivering pins was one I simply couldn't pass up.

Jed Allan

Over the course of the show's nearly 90 shows, which were all shot at a two-lane alley constructed in the studios of KTTV in Los Angeles, our celebrity bowlers included, among others, Steve Allen, Brenda Vaccaro, the kids from *The Brady Bunch*, Richard Dawson, Sammy Davis, Jr., Phyllis Diller, Michael Douglas, Sid Caesar, Tom Kennedy, Wink Martindale, Jayne Meadows, Roy Rogers, Cesar Romero, William Shatner, McLean Stevenson, Lyle Waggoner, and Adam West.

Many of these celebs were surprisingly good, though some were incredibly bad. Perhaps my worst bowlers ever were none other than The Lennon Sisters, who though they could most likely have charmed those ten pins down on the strength of their harmonious voices alone, simply couldn't knock down a pin to save their lives. Their best score was eighty-nine, for all four of them.

The honor of second worst bowler in the history of the show, however, most certainly goes to good friend—and admittedly rotten bowler—Robert Clary, best known as Corporal Louis LeBeau from *Hogan's Heroes*. He bowled somewhere in the 70s, and I don't mean the year.

Apparently, there were no bowling alleys in France …

… and Longer Grudges

There was no doubt that *Celebrity Bowling* was more lucrative than *Lassie*. Much more lucrative, in part because there was no agent involved. American Federation of Television and Radio Artists statutes require a "per show" payment as opposed to a "per day" payment, which meant that in one weekend, while an entire season's bumper crop of thirty shows were taped, I could make a whopping $50,000. Naturally, this was something the producers didn't exactly agree with. They would have preferred for me to receive $1,500 per day, as opposed to per episode.

But what can I say?

The law's the law …

Certainly, the days were long. Ad-libbing with Steve Allen one minute and cast members from the *Mod Squad* the next was an exercise in pop culture credibility that taxed yours truly to no end. But I learned quickly what, and what not, to ask.

The stars were usually happy to be on the show and many of us knew each other from guest roles on other TV shows and movies, or soon would as a result of our endless networking on the set.

It was a lot like *Hollywood Squares.*

In a bowling alley.

All weekend long—and no script …

Naturally, the producers, Don Gregory and Joe Siegman, were kicking themselves over the pay scale. Dishing out $50,000 for three days' work is hard for anybody to do, but apparently even harder for Joe.

As a matter of fact, Joe still owes me $4,000 for several unpaid episodes of that show.

Joe, are you listening?

That's okay, Joe.

I know where you live …

The Boob Tube Boom

If TV had boomed in the 60s, it quickly became a meteor on fire in the 70s. As both daytime and nighttime dramas saw a surge in ratings and viewers raced home to catch up on the exploits of their latest television stars, Hollywood producers quickly began ramping up to speed to meet their viewing public's nearly insatiable demand for all things television.

The early 70s saw a gold rush of hour-long nightly dramas, usually built around a star cast of two to four recognizable celebrities who showed up every week wearing cowboy hats, army uniforms, curly red hair and maracas, or a leash for their favorite celebrity pooch.

Timing had always been one of my strong points. Looking out onto a crowded dance floor and spotting my future bride to running into Broadway producers on the streets of Manhattan, I'd somehow always managed to be in the right place in the right time. Fortunately for me, the 70s would be no different.

Professionally, I was swinging. With Broadway, live soaps, and a big picture under my belt, I was in the right place at the right time as America's focus turned squarely toward their living room television sets. *Big Valley* had led to *Lassie*, *Lassie* had led to *Celebrity Bowling*, *Celebrity Bowling* had led to a resume that many young actors just arriving in Tinsel Town would die for.

Though I was far from a household name, I felt that I was just what casting directors were looking for at that moment: Solid, reliable, dependable, likeable, but most of all, *lucky*. Then again, I also knew it had more to do with just sheer luck.

Sheer luck was a part of everything in this business.

Acting to me had always been more about the craft than the cash, and though I often donned tie and tails at gigs like the IBM Pavilion to put bread on the table, I never let a part, a play, or a paycheck pass without exhibiting my fair share of that other "p" word: Professionalism.

I'd seen one too many a Buddy Hackett in my day, playing the star bit to the hilt and causing delays, bruised egos, and burned bridges in his wake. I made sure to always show up on time, know my lines, listen to direction, improvise when necessary, and do just what was needed *when* it was needed. As a result, producers usually called me more than once.

The producers at the hit show *Adam–12* were very kind to me …

Adam–12

Though it wasn't the first television series to portray cops, *Adam–12* did appear to be the first show to realistically portray the ups and downs of being a Los Angeles police officer in the 70s. Many attribute this to the fact that its creator and executive producer was none other than famous TV cop himself, *Dragnet*'s venerable Jack Webb.

Of course the success of the show hinges on the writing and production values, but the key to *Adam–12* was the relationship between the two stars. The eternally young Kent McCord played Officer Jim Reed while his more veteran and down to earth partner, Officer Pete Malloy, was portrayed by Martin Milner.

I got to know Martin, or "Marty" as most people referred to him, better than most when I played Charles Jensen on a guest role in an episode titled simply "Bank Robbery" in April of 1970.

By now I knew my way as well as most did around the set of a popular television series, but each one is different—some good, some not so good—and the set of *Adam–12* was one of the most professionally illuminating I've had the joys of experiencing to date.

I like to think I fit in, and that fact seems to be reflected by the close friendship that formed between Marty Milner and myself, not to mention the fact that I guested in several more episodes of *Adam–12* over the following years, including "Anatomy of a 415," "Hot Shot," "L.A. International," and "Reno West," a two-parter.

Marty was just a "regular guy" who happened to find himself in front of millions of viewers each week. Off the set, however, he was as kind and gentle a soul as you could find, in Hollywood or anywhere else for that matter.

He and his beautiful wife Judy lived on an avocado farm in Del Mar, California and Toby and I loved to escape our house in the suburban valley and get back to nature on Marty's sprawling acreage.

But farming wasn't Marty's only hobby. His passion for fly-fishing has sent him to secluded fishin' holes all over the world to test his angling skills. It even got him a paying gig: Today Marty co-hosts a very popular syndicated radio show about fishing called *Let's Talk Hook-up* based in California.

Marty and I and Toby and Judy even did a game show together starring Bert Convey called "Tattle Tales." We kind of lost touch as the years went by, but he and Judy were very dear to Toby and me during those days.

Beating up a Legend

The 70s seemed to be a decade obsessed with cops and robbers. At least on television, anyway. From my first appearance on *Adam–12*, I appeared as a guest star on several notable cop dramas, from *CHiPs* to *McMillan and Wife* to *Mannix* to *Columbo*. But none was as hip, cool, or memorable as my stint on what was arguably the 70s hottest, most unique show, the *Mod Squad*.

What the Beatles had done for fashion, grammar, and pop culture in the 60s, the *Mod Squad* did for all of the above in the 70s. From hairstyles and bell bottoms to sunglasses and buzz words like "solid," Peggy Lipton, Clarence Williams III, and Michael Cole—Julie, Linc, and Pete respectively—changed the "cop show" formula forever.

Many actors guested on the popular series, from Harrison Ford to Richard Pryor, from Louis Gossett, Jr. to Della Reese, but I was lucky enough to appear with the best of the best: Sammy Davis, Jr.

I had long been a fan of this multi-faceted, ultra-talented superstar and, though I doubt *he'd* remember our first "meeting," it was one I'll not soon forget. The year was 1956 and I was a struggling student at the Pasadena Playhouse. But struggling or no, I was too close to Las Vegas not to go and catch a living legend on stage when he came to town that long, hot summer.

It cost nine dollars for a room at the New Frontier Hotel that year, and $7.50 for a ticket to see Sammy Davis, Jr. live and onstage. He sang, he danced, he played the drums, he played the trumpet, he did it all. And made it look effortless.

On a stage, the man could do no wrong.

Unfortunately, in the casino after the show, I could do nothing *but.* I started by winning a few hands of blackjack, and ended losing. Losing big. To the tune of $2,200. In 1956! I had to call my dad and have him wire me the money all the way from Bronx. Needless to say, it wasn't a chore he relished.

"Enjoy it, son," he said gravely. "Cause I'll *never* do this again …"

He'd sent just enough to cover my checks, pay my hotel tab, and get back to Pasadena without a pair of cuffs dangling from my wrists. I stayed away from Vegas for years after that, not returning until the early 70s when I could afford to lose my own money. Which I inevitably did. (And continue to do to this day …)

It was a hard lesson, but not one learned in vain. The loss, the shame, the chagrin, it had all been worth it to see Sammy Davis, Jr. live and in person.

And now I was being hired to beat him up!

On October 20, 1970, I appeared in "The Song of Willie" as a vicious mobster who takes a savage delight in beating up the diminutive but talented "Willie," played by Sammy. Now, Sammy and I didn't share a whole lot of screen time on the popular TV series, though in the final product it looks like I took particular glee in pounding him into the pavement.

In reality, I spent most of my time shadow boxing with the cameraman. Or, more specifically, the camera itself. It's been done before.

In this particular scene, the director wanted the audience to see what Sammy Davis, Jr. might have witnessed as I, said vicious mobster, beat the hell out of him. The camera of course was held low since Sammy was so small and I had to hit down on the camera it took all day but what a day that was. And what a sweet, generous man Sammy was. We crossed each other's paths many times before his death, and he always made me feel like I was the star.

Coulda Been Columbo

Before a show becomes a series, studio execs like to see what it will feel like, look like, sound like, who will work with who, who won't, the works. Enter what is known as "the pilot."

The pilot is an episode before the rest of the episodes. A mini-movie, designed to win the "hearts and minds" of even the stodgiest studio exec. Great care is taken to stay true to the creator's vision, while also pulling out all the stops for the big wigs.

It's always fun to work on a pilot, as the hope is ever present that you might just land a regular spot on the show once, and if, it becomes a weekly series. Such was the case with *Columbo*, whose pilot episode, "Ransom for a Dead Man" premiered on March 1, 1971 with yours truly playing a character named "Gene."

Though the pilot obviously won over the studio heads and eventually got the green light, making an overnight star out of its lovably grizzled industry veteran, Peter Falk, the episode is notable to me for a slightly less hygienic reason.

While riding around in a car with co-star Harry Gardino during one particular scene, we were required to eat while we drove. Unbeknownst to me, and apparently the rest of the crew, there was a tiny smidgeon of food on the corner of my lip.

Usually, under such circumstances, someone from the set will call "Cut" and come over and wipe you off. Not so on the *Columbo* pilot. There the food remained, stuck on my lip, for the entire scene. Even when the dailies came back, no one apparently caught it. And thus am I immortalized forever in the annals of series television with egg on my face.

Literally …

Love, 70s Style

On September 29, 1969 the country got its first dose of *Love, American Style*. And, although the show itself never ranked above number twenty-five in the Nielsen Ratings, America stayed hooked until the last episode aired some 108 episodes later on Friday, January 11, 1974.

The show's premise was simple: Cute, clever, some might call them "bold" for the time, stories about common people finding love in all walks of life. The show was a popular one for ABC on Friday nights, airing from ten p.m. to eleven p.m., just late enough for adults to have drinks and dinner and return home and put the kids to bed before it came on.

The hour-long show featured two or three stories of *Love, American Style*. Also, on the broadcasts, short "blackout sketches" would be shown in-between segments. In the middle of the 70s toward the end of the run of the show, I became one of the "blackout players." As so often happens in television, my opportunity came as a result of someone else's good news. In this case, the executive producer's brother.

Stuart Margolin was a popular blackout player on *Love, American Style* from its earliest incarnation in the late 60s. But when Stuart wanted to move on and eventually got the chance to play James Garner's sidekick in the hot new 70s series, *Rockford Files*, a new blackout player was needed.

Stuart's brother, Arnold Margolin, who just happened to be one of the show's executive producers, hired me to replace him. All this happened after I had already appeared in several episodes of *Love, American Style* through the years.

My first appearance was in Episode 65, aptly titled "Love and the Bathtub." The show's tagline, "Wedding-day slapstick when the bride's toe gets stuck in the faucet," hardly describes the delight I got when slipping into a bubbly bathtub opposite sultry Julie Newmar, best known for her role as

Cat Woman on the *Batman* television series. The episode aired on January 21, 1972 and required much appeasing on my part as Toby and I watched the sexy scene in our own bedroom.

Up until now, my female co-stars had been Lassie and Barbara Stanwyck. Cat Woman, naked, in a bathtub, was quite another story altogether. But Toby took it like a pro. Then again, she had to.

The show was already in the can.

And there was more to come …

"Love and the Sensuous Twin," starring yours truly with Sandra Dee and Roddy McDowall was followed shortly thereafter by another guest appearance in "Love and the Spaced Out Chick."

My favorite appearance on the *Love, American Style* series was also my last. "Love and the Hand Maiden" starred Michele Lee and James Callahan. Playing against type, of course, I was cast as a pig of a man who wanted nothing more than to ravage every beautiful woman he came in contact with. My infatuation with co-star Michele Lee was no different.

Except, of course, in the bedroom …

"A model who is willing to remove everything—except her gloves" was how the episode was described. So I spent the entire episode trying to get her gloves off. The clothes were easy, but the gloves, they were something else. I became desperate to see her hands. So desperate at the end of the show I asked her to marry me. Why, you might ask? If you can't figure that out, sell your TV.

This was just one of many clever episodes I enjoyed from the popular late-night TV show, whether I was in them or not. The country agreed, and *Love, American Style* went on to appear in syndication everywhere from the Oxygen Network to Nick-at-Nite. I'm sure, if you look hard enough, you'll see it playing somewhere right now.

I have nothing but fond memories of my stints on *Love, American Style*, but I'm sure my good friend and former executive producer, Jim Parker, might not be so generous with his own recollections. Despite the show's success, its Golden Globe nomination, and its profits from syndication over the years, Jim left the show penniless after the studio's "creative financing" department robbed him of his ten percent of the cut.

Jed Allan

Maybe he's ready for a sequel: *Betrayal, Hollywood Style …*

And Now, Sitting in for Ted Baxter

The hit parade of high profile guest appearances on some of the decade's most popular shows continued as the 70s steamed ahead at full tilt. *The Mary Tyler Moore Show* first aired in September of 1970 and ran for seven years on CBS. Before the decade was even over, it remained one of the most popular and acclaimed sitcoms of the 70s.

Mary Tyler Moore. Ed Asner. Gavin MacLeod. Ted Knight. Cloris Leachman. Valerie Harper. Betty White. The star power from that show still reverberates through the industry today. I was asked to guest star on Episode 33 of the hit TV show, "And Now, Sitting in for Ted Baxter." Ted Baxter, of course, was the wonderfully talented Ted Knight, who sadly passed away a few years back.

I fell in love with the script as easily as I did the warm, giving, and generous actors who peopled the MTM set: "Ted is forced to take a vacation and the anchorman hired to sit in for him becomes a huge success." The anchorman? Yours truly. Or, in this case, a character named Rod Porter who was in every way the antithesis of the silver-haired, short, stocky, Baxter, played by the irrepressible Ted Knight. Baxter was so insecure he didn't take a vacation, hiding instead around the studio hoping my character would flop and he'd get his job back.

Meeting Ed Asner was a thrill. Calling him my good friend to this day is even more so. But perhaps the most lasting friendship I formed on that popular television show was with its future *Love Boat* captain, Gavin MacLeod, who just the other day sent me a script for a play he wanted to do. I love Gavin, but I didn't like the play.

What the guest shot did for my visibility was nothing compared to the lasting friendships it gave me. Looking back, there's no question which was more important.

Guest Shots & Flop Sweat

As the 70s marched on, there was no doubt that I was riding high on a wave of popular appearances and visible series guest roles. But despite the growing resume and influential list of powerful new friends, I was still living the vagabond life.

Toby was a joy and my three boys were my strength, and on the surface I'm sure I was the envy of many a young actor. "I had it all," as they say in this biz, and the judgment wasn't far off from the truth.

On the surface, anyway …

But many a morning I woke in a flop sweat, covered in perspiration and my chest pounding above my racing heart wondering, "Who will I pay today? Where will the money come from?" Guest roles are impressive, personally rewarding, and professionally advancing, but hardly enough to retire on, let alone feed your wife and kids.

I had established quite a reputation for myself, had made all the right moves, knew all the right people, lived in the right neighborhood, wore the right clothes, appeared on all the right shows, and still I wondered how I'd pay our mortgage next month.

In the industry trade mags, I was the "guy to look out for."

In reality, I was broke …

When it got too bad, I would share my feelings with Toby. But far from urging me to "get a real job," as many "Hollywood Wives" of her era were wont to do, she always reminded me that, "Before we get really broke, something comes along. It always has, it always will. Just be patient …"

On the scorecard of life lessons, Toby was batting 1,000.

Before I knew it, I would hit a home run …

Like Sands Through the Hourglass …

According to www.SoapCity.com: "In its thirty-seven years, *Days of Our Lives* has generated numerous Emmy Awards and nominations, as well as numerous *Soap Opera Digest* Awards and People's Choice Awards. The show's success derives from its consistent commitment to excellence in writing and storytelling—supported by a diverse ensemble of performers—and an uncanny knack for anticipating viewer interests. From demonic possessions and baby switches to exciting teen stories and classic love triangles, *Days of our Lives* remains a perennial favorite among viewers of all ages …"

I knew all of this already, of course. A veteran of two soap operas by now, and live ones at that, there wasn't a daytime series that hadn't popped up on my acting radar at one time or another. Still, when my agent landed me an audition for the role of "Doug Williams" in late 1972, I went into it thinking either way, success or failure, it would still be a "win/win" situation for me.

I'd already been down the road of daytime drama, and had only been mildly impressed with what I had found waiting for me at that particular fork in the highway. And now I was on a roll in the nighttime, increasingly playing larger and larger parts on bigger and bigger shows. Landing a lead on a daytime drama would be full of as many pros as there were cons.

At the time, I knew I was straddling two worlds: Daytime and nighttime. And yet the world I really wanted, the brass ring just out of reach, was the same that eluded so many television actors of my era: Feature films.

Working on *Ice Station Zebra* had been a sheer delight, and I yearned for more of the same. And yet, somehow, some way, the big parts always eluded me. And thus I shuttled from soundstage to soundstage, meeting larger than life television stars who, likewise, were hoping for their big break as well.

The one that would launch them onto the big screen …

And perhaps it was that "I don't give a damn" attitude that helped me beat out ninety-nine of the 100 other male actors who showed up for the *Days of Our Lives* audition during one week in 1972. When all was said and done, the part of Doug would be decided between myself and another actor, Bill Hayes.

When Bill got the part, I must confess, my "win/win" philosophy didn't exactly help keep me from feeling like I'd just "lost." In a big way. Still, the setback was only temporary and, besides, I had another guest shot to prepare for.

Still, as I bounced from guest shot to guest shot, I couldn't help but grow weary of my gypsy ways. Never knowing where my next paycheck was coming from had been exciting at first, now it was just a pain in the ass. Not being able to buy a new washing machine for Toby or having to put off braces for one of the boys wasn't exciting, it was a drag.

So when the producers of *Days of Our Lives* called me back three months later and asked me if I would like to play four shows as the lawyer handling Julie's divorce, I said, "Sure, what the hell …"

Obviously, the producers had kept me in mind from my recent audition and found a part for me in the end, albeit a small one. You never know what can happen when you do a daytime show. Talk about your win/win.

To my great delight, and good fortune, those four performances as politician and lawyer, Don Craig , "…son of Amelia Craig, brother of Angela and Paolo Craig; father of Betsy and D.J. Craig, adoptive father of Donna Craig; ex-husband of Marlena Evans and Liz Chandler …" turned into almost thirteen years.

Some of the best years of my life …

… So Are the *Days of Our Lives*

My character on *Days of Our Lives*, Don Craig, was the perfect male soap opera lead: Nice guy, charming, successful, a wealthy attorney who dabbled in politics—and beautiful women. Need I say more?

Well, actually, there *was* more. Compared to today's male leads, Don Craig was a genuinely nice guy, perhaps even part of a dying breed: A true gentleman. He didn't pursue the women, in fact, they pursued him. And he was the easiest guy in the world to play. *If* you had any amount of charm at all, that is. And charm?

Charm I had coming out of my ass.

Now *that's* charm …

I was impressed with the *Days* set from the very beginning. Walking into one of the most successful daytime dramas in history isn't easy, but both the cast and crew welcomed me warmly and I owe this fact in great part, I'm sure, to actor Bill Hayes for paving my way from day one.

Having lost the role of Doug Williams to Bill some months earlier had proved to be a blessing in disguise. Now our reunion was not only personally satisfying, but professionally rewarding as well. Bill greased my way onto the set with humility and charity, and made my stay there as friendly as possible.

Naturally, I tried to give Don Craig a life beyond the mere pages of his daily script. My reward for the effort turned out to be two-fold. As my role on *Days* grew more permanent, I waited for the dreaded contract to come down from the production office.

All soap leads are "contract players," signed on for a year, if not years at a time, and while I welcomed the steady work, I knew that to sign a contract for daytime when my nighttime career was seemingly taking off would take me out of the mainstream of film and nighttime TV. I knew there was definitely a bias against daytime actors starring at night. I never wanted to hear the dreaded phrase, "Naw, he's daytime, not nighttime."

But for three long years I would have my cake, and eat it, too. Producers weren't sure whether or not to keep Don Craig around, and thus avoided giving me a contract to sign. As such, I freelanced for three seasons, enjoying the steady paycheck of weekly soap work as well as the occasional guest spot on such shows as *Kojak* and *The Streets of San Francisco*.

Life, it seemed, was good.

And it was bound to get better any day now …

Daytime Blues?

By the time I finally signed a contract for *Days of Our Lives*, it was 1975 and half the decade had already passed. And what a great five years it had been. Those flop sweat mornings were finally gone, replaced instead by early trips to the NBC Studio at 3000 Alameida in Burbank.

Days were very early. Back then to beat the congestion of traffic out of our home in the San Fernando Valley, you had to be on the road by five-thirty in the morning. Fortunately, I had to be at the studio for a "dry block" by six.

Unfortunately, this meant I was up at four-thirty to shower, dress, and drive the thirty minutes to the studio and be there on time, if not early. I let Toby sleep, she had three little monsters to get to school, and thus I began my day alone.

During a dry block, the actors in a scene would move around in a room, but not on stage. We'd trade lines, make cuts, find our marks, followed by a dress rehearsal, all the while rehearsing our lines.

Please, Spell the Name Right

After the dry block came a more formal walk-through on stage, followed by a dress blocking, followed by a dress rehearsal, and maybe another walk-through rehearsal, to solidify things depending on who was the director that day. All the while running lines with each other in-between rehearsals. All this before we went to tape somewhere around two or three each afternoon. Four five times we read, walked, and blocked our parts, in various stages of hair, makeup, and costume, at various locations around the studio.

Over the years, fans always ask me the same thing: "How did you learn all those lines?" But memorizing the lines wasn't actually the hard part. Don't get me wrong, it was challenging. A lead in a popular soap opera can be in as many as four to five scenes a day, containing two to three pages of dialogue each. Add it up, that's up to fifteen to twenty pages of dialogue per day, sometimes more. Four to five days per week.

It can get daunting, and there *are* cue cards, but using a cue card is often as hazardous as memorizing your lines in the first place. It's almost impossible to "read a cue" without getting caught.

Although they're usually in the middle of the two farthest cameras, so as to avoid that "looking straight into the camera effect," but the reason people get "caught" looking at the cue cards is because it's obvious they're not thinking about their character's actions, it's obvious they're *looking* for a cue card.

The trick, then, was just to memorize your lines in the first place. That, and pay attention to what's going on in the scene. Over the years I learned a number of techniques for buying time while I recalled a line that was hazy or elusive.

I called it my "thinking process." I'd take a dramatic pause, make it look like I was "thinking" about something the other character had just said, and inevitably the line, or something similar, would eventually come to me.

If my thinking process didn't work, I'd eventually scan the room for a cue card, but only as a last resort, and I'd make it look natural. Sometimes I'd take a drink, or straighten my tie, or use some other mechanism to make the pause look natural. Then I'd see the cue in passing, and eventually come up with the line.

The greatest thing for stopping the use of this "crutch" was when, years later in a new show, after a new executive producer came in and took away the cards, I realized that I'd never needed them in the first place.

I got to the point where I could learn my lines the day of the taping. I'd get the essence of the scene the night before, learn what it was about, and commit the lines to memory the day of the episode.

Still, memorizing lines paled in comparison to delivering what I call the "emotional goods" day after day. Even a casual fan of daytime TV notices the wide range of emotions an actor is forced to convey from scene to scene. The light stuff almost anybody can do, it's the heavy stuff that takes its toll. How do you find tears in the middle of the day, when things are going great?

And things *were* going great …

Smell the Roses, Honey …

I can honestly say that doing *Days* was a walk in the park. The lines, the scenes, the read throughs, the rehearsals, the commitments, please don't ever think I took a minute of it for granted or didn't appreciate my good fortune at what was previously a very tenuous time in my life.

In fact, aside from getting up at five in the morning to miss freeway traffic, life was a breeze. However, as time went on and *Days* became more of a routine and less of a novelty, I do admit that I had growing concerns over being typecast as a daytime actor.

The fears, it seemed, were warranted. Actors, like any other employees, crave variety. I was grateful for the role on *Days*, for the world it opened up to me, for the financial security. Who wouldn't be?

But at the same time I felt that just as I was getting on a role with nighttime television or even film rolls, *Days* came along and threatened to stymie that lucky streak. Would I have rather done a nighttime television series? Of course. Who wouldn't? Would I have rather dabbled in film roles? Naturally.

Who wouldn't? Like everyone else, I'd heard one too many a casting director or producer take one look at an actor's head shot and complain, "We can't use this guy. He's daytime, not nighttime …"

Please, Spell the Name Right

Whenever I got tired or complained about not having the time to audition for nighttime or film roles, however, Toby was always there to keep me on the straight and narrow.

"Honey," she said, "Jed, for crying out loud, please bite your tongue. Remember the flop sweat days? Those weren't so very long ago, and now you're working steady and making very good money. How can you possibly complain? Honey, *please* smell the roses …"

So I thought of all those flop sweat mornings, how I'd wondered where my next paycheck was coming from, how my kids had had to wait for things, how Toby and I used to fight about money all the time.

I knew the statistics, perhaps even better than anyone: Of the over 50,000 actors with a SAG card, only five to ten percent made a living from their craft.

The numbers were sobering.

The lesson was learned.

I never complained again. Well, *almost* never.

Smell the roses, honey …

Kissing Contest

By 1976 I had been on *Days of Our Lives* for four years and had seen my share of comas, incest, violence, drama, laughter, births, deaths, and tears. And that was all in one week. (Just kidding.) Don Craig was now an established character and I had a signed contract in my pocket that said so.

Bill Hayes, aka Doug Williams, wife of Julie Olson Banning Anderson, father of Hope Williams, con man, lounge singer at Sergio's, and owner of popular Doug's place, was not only a trusted friend but respected colleague, and by now we were both firmly entrenched in the *Days of Our Lives* family, for better or worse.

I had the role, I had the clothes, I had the emotions stoked. Now it was time for a romance, and for that to happen—I would need a leading lady. I did double duty the week they hired my love interest, reading with fifteen finalists, part of fifty-plus who auditioned. All of them beautiful, all of them talented, all of them lovely, enchanting women.

136

Jed Allan

In the end, however, six of them remained no more talented, lovely, and enchanting than the rest, but what the producers picked. With these select women, I would do a scene. And as one of these lovely ladies was to be the future Mrs. Don Craig, it would naturally be … a love scene.

A love scene being, of course, a fancy term for a "kissing contest." After all, that's what it all boiled down to. All of these lovely gals could act, they were all beautiful women, and all that was left now was one vital element: Chemistry.

Bring on the sugar …

For the life of me, I can't remember the names of the other five women I kissed that day. But after it was all said and done, the producers and I sat down and whittled the list down to the top three. But three was still two to many, and so the question became, "Of these three women, who would you pick as Don Craig's love interest?"

I thought long and hard before answering. One woman had smelled the best, kissed the best, tasted the best. Only one woman, in the end, did what you were supposed to do in a love scene: And that's turn your partner on.

"I'd choose Deidre," I said without hesitation. "She's the best kisser … and she's got a sense of humor."

Headed for a Fall

And so it was that, in 1976, Don Craig met and fell in love with Dr. Marlena Evans, to be played by *Days* newcomer … Deidre Hall. Like Bill Hayes before me and Jed Allan before her, Deidre Hall was welcomed onto the *Days* set with open arms, and remains there to this day.

Big things were in store for Don and Marlena, not the least of which included a twin sister named Samantha, who she had never met, a forced exile in the sanitarium at Salem's famous Bayview Hospital, and a child who would later died from SIDS, perhaps one of the first socially conscious acts made by soap opera writers to date.

Much has been written about Don and Marlena, even more has been said. Suffice it to say that Deidre Hall was then and is now a dear, dear friend and has always been the classiest of ladies. As charming as she is beautiful, as intelligent as she is gorgeous, as humble, not necessarily, but I'd be hard-pressed to find any dirt to dish on this soap opera diva.

Sorry, gang …

Then again … in December of 1977, Don decided to run for state senate. However, in 1978 the newspapers started a smear campaign against Don. When Don's old girlfriend Lorraine Temple saw his picture in the paper she returned to Salem to tell Don about the daughter he never knew he had, Donna. The papers got a hold of this story and used it to tarnish his reputation, but Marlena stood by Don.

Lorraine eventually left town, but Donna stayed behind. Donna had trouble adjusting to her new life with her father and his bride to be Marlena. On the day Don was to marry Marlena, their wedding was interrupted when Donna threatened to jump off a nearby building. Don and Marlena ran to her rescue, but in the process Don fell from the building and injured his leg—and also his spleen. Don's injuries forced him to drop out of his race for the senate.

It also caused my character, Don Craig, to be hard of hearing. (From a fall? Hey, remember, this is a soap opera. Stranger things have happened …) For six months I was a cripple, and five days a week during that entire time, Deidre Hall spent endless hours trying to trick me into responding to verbal cues and throw me out of character as a deaf man with a broken leg and punctured spleen.

Every dress rehearsal for six months Deidre sounded like a bull in a china shop, dropping books, slamming doors, shouting my name, muttering obscenities, all in a vain attempt to get me to drop character and "hear" her.

Long before she was ever possessed, Deidre Hall was a little devil.

But a cute pain in the ass at times. However, she was so much fun to work with, a little pain never hurt anybody …

What it Means to be Number One

Soap operas would be nothing without their fans, and in turn fans would be lost without their soap opera magazines. For years magazines like *Soap Opera*

Digest and *Soap Opera Weekly* have kept readers informed, and actors popular, by detailing every coma, wedding, divorce, death, birth, and kiss to
cross the airwaves during eleven to two o'clock on one of the big three.

One of the most popular features of all such magazines is the "top ten
list" appearing in each. Top Ten Actress. Top Ten Villain. Top Ten Poison.
Top Ten Escape. Top Ten Romance. You name it, if it's on soaps, there's a
top ten list for it. And, for two straight years, my Bill Hayes had been at the
top of the Top Ten list of Actors.

I'd never been one for contests, games, or rankings, and neither, for that
matter, had Bill. But it's hard to ignore your standings once you get to
number one. Still, Bill Hayes took it all in stride. There wasn't an ounce of
ego in the man, not when he was #100, not when he was number ten, not
even when he was number one. For two years in a row.

Not long after he'd climbed the height of the rankings, my name appeared on the same list. Pretty low, at first. But each week it got a little
higher. I must admit it was addictive, following the rankings, but I tried to
take a cue from Bill's gentle humility and, too, took the rapid ascent in
stride.

But one day Bill came tearing down the halls of the studio, dragging his
Soap Opera Magazine along like a racing form with a winning steed and
screaming, "Guess who's number one? Guess who's number one?"

"You are," I said, marveling at the delayed reaction. After all, he'd been
number one for two years now.

"You are," he said proudly, as if either of us had anything to do with it.
He shoved the magazine in my face and, sure enough, there I was at number one. And where was old Bill? He'd finally slipped to number two.
"Congratulations," he said earnestly, sincerely, proud as a new father, beaming like he'd just won the lottery. "You must be thrilled."

"Are you crazy?" I asked, waiting for the punch line. "I just took your
spot!"

He didn't even blink. His smile remained fixed throughout the day. "My
big day" he called it, never giving a thought to himself. Never in a million
years could I imagine being as magnanimous and kind on the day someone
took *my* spot after two long years. What a guy, what a guy.

I'd stay number one, or in the top ten, for the next eighty-five months. As far as I'm concerned, Bill Hayes is *still* number one …

Drag is a Drag

Despite the glitz, the glamour, the beauty, the clothes, the opulence, the adoration, being in a soap opera is a job like any other. You hear the alarm clock, you stumble through the shower, you race to beat rush hour, you say your lines, you hit your mark, you take your breath mints, you kiss beautiful women, you wear expensive, tailored clothes, and you leave the make believe behind and come home to your beautiful wife and three kids.

Okay, so I never said it was chopped liver.

But it was still a job …

And, like any job, some days were better than others. I fondly recall a week where we were hosting a Telethon and doing a riff on a Groucho Marx film. As luck would have it, I was tapped to dress as a woman and play society dame Margaret Dumont to Frances Reid's impeccable Groucho.

I couldn't have looked uglier. Bad wig, bad dress, bad fit, bad shoes, worse lighting, I can't imagine a soul who took it—or me, for that matter—seriously that day. Until, that is, I flew to New York to attend an awards ceremony a week later and ran into a producer at the bar.

The meeting started out friendly enough. "Congratulations on your award," he said magnanimously, raising his glass in a toast. "But don't ever do a woman again. People will think you're gay and you won't get any work …"

An awkward silence filled his sober warning. I looked him in the eye, trying to gauge if he was pulling my leg or not. His expression was as cold as the ice in his glass. For him, this was no joking matter.

"Are you kidding me?" I asked, hardly believing my ears and trying my best to keep my trembling hands around my rocks glass—and off of his throat. "Get out of my face before I say, or do, something we'll both regret …"

"Who would say such a thing?" I wondered as I watched him scramble away to his seat. But then it dawned on me: The only person who could ever say such a thing, *imagine* such a thing, surely had to be someone still in the closet.

I wonder if he ever opened the door …

The Man from Clover Grove

Days of Our Lives would dominate *my* life for the next dozen years, but along the way old friends and co-stars would drop in to offer not only their friendship, but professional opportunities as well.

My role on *Ice Station Zebra* had been limited to the sixty-five different ways I was able to say "thin ice," but I'd warmed to my many co-stars immediately and still communicated with many of them on a regular basis.

Willy "Bill" Hillman had been an actor on *Ice*, but was now a writer and director. In the mid-70s he was putting both to good use in *The Man From Clover Grove*, a G–rated family flick he had written and was now directing.

Bill was a loyal friend, and looked closest to him when casting for the film. He'd hired fellow *Ice* alum Ron Masek as Claude Raintree—Ron also sings the title song—and cast me as "The Hippie." It was one of the few feature films I did during the 70s, but the closeness and camaraderie on the set made it feel like a high school reunion.

One I wished would never end …

Rent-a-Yenta

It's long been said that behind every successful man is a woman, and to be sure Toby had been through thick and thin with me, and never once complained. Her enthusiasm was unmatched in Hollywood and her humor second to none, even in a room full of the day's brightest comics.

But now it was my turn to be the man behind the successful woman.

Or, in this case, the successful *yenta* …

Yenta is Yiddish for matchmaker. Literally, the word signifies "one who puts things together." Let it be said that Toby had always been good at "putting things together." From decorating a basement apartment beneath the land of nudist winemakers until it looked like something out of a glossy Home Décor magazine to raising three boys who would give zoo trainers the fits, Toby had done it all with a smile—and one hand tied behind her back.

She was renowned for the elaborate parties she gave, the thoughtful gifts she handed over during the holidays, the lavishly decorated cakes she *bought*, notice I didn't say baked, the appropriate music she chose, it didn't matter what she put together, it always ended up the same way: Flawless.

As the 70s steamed forward, it seemed the Brown family could do no wrong. Don Craig was on *Days of Our Lives* four to five days a week, and occasionally gracing nighttime TV on shows like *Eischied* and the *Marcus Welby, MD*. And as our boys grew, though they'd still yet to mellow, Toby had more and more time to put things together for more and more people.

She was often accompanied by her trusted friend and soon to be business partner, Lila Green. One day, after throwing yet another successful birthday party for yet another satisfied friend, Toby and Lila got an idea: Why not charge people for all the hard work and effort that went into these lavish affairs?

It was an idea that stuck. The two gals, born salesmen, er, saleswomen, quickly set on the name: Rent-a-Yenta. They made business cards, got a catering license, and immediately set about letting their friends know that they were, literally, "in business."

Soon Toby was working just as hard, if not harder, than I was. Rent-a-Yenta was the right idea at the right time, and caught on like a flash. The girls were racing all around town, working for both the rich and famous and the average Joe alike.

When Sammy Davis, Jr. wanted a bar mitzvah (albeit belated), Toby found him a rabbi. When Bill Cosby wanted a woman to jump out of a cake for his birthday party in Las Vegas, it wasn't just Toby who arranged it, it was Toby jumping *out* of it! (Although the cake had somehow gotten turned around and, instead of greeting the Coz with a birthday smile, she popped out backside first … until the cake could get turned around, that is!)

As business boomed, I knew it wouldn't be long before my services were needed …

Jed Allan

Special Delivery

One of Rent-a-Yenta's more popular services was its lavish Thanksgiving dinners, delivered hot and ready to eat, with all the fixings. So popular, in fact, that one year there were too many dinners … and not enough drivers.

It was time to hire extra help.

And Toby looked no further than her very own living room.

"Oh Jed," I can still hear her calling in a voice that really said, "I need your help even though you'd rather be sitting in your easy chair watching the ball game." And help I did. Not only my services, but my car was requisitioned that fateful Thanksgiving Day in 1976 as I headed throughout the San Fernando Valley—and beyond—to deliver turkey dinners to folks too lazy, or too busy, to cook for themselves.

The task would have been much simpler years earlier, when my face wasn't being broadcast throughout millions of homes five days a week. But now I was a contract regular, sucking face with Deidre Hall on a weekly basis, and as luck would have it that day it wasn't the men of the house answering the door when their homemade turkey dinner arrived.

There I'd be, Don Craig, live and in person, holding a wrapped assortment of holiday treats, not to mention an entire turkey. There would be the woman of the house, trying to put the face with the Rent-a-Yenta label all over the turkey.

"Aren't you?" would ask said housewife.

"Oh no," the deliveryman would lie. "But I get that a lot."

"Yes you are," would insist the housewife, calling into the house for reinforcements should any other soap fans be in attendance.

"No, really, I'm not," the deliveryman would lie again, slowly backing away before hordes of nieces, sisters, daughters, grandmothers, and aunts could deliver expert testimony in the doorway. "We just look alike. Happy Thanksgiving…"

And then it was off to the next house, only to repeat the performance. I don't know which was worse. Thinking Don Craig had just delivered your Thanksgiving turkey and not believing your own eyes, or thinking Don Craig had just delivered your Thanksgiving turkey and *believing* your own eyes … but not remembering to grab your camera until he was already driving away.

One time the woman who answered the door said, "I know you, you're, you're, you're…"

I was so tired of it all I said, "Yes, I'm Jed Allan."

"No you're not," she answered, "I know who Jed *Allan* is, you're, you're, you're…"

I slowly turned around and faded into the sunset, saying to myself, "I'm Jed Allan, Jed Allan, Jed Allan …"

Hot Lips Was a Hot Ticket First …

As if Toby and I weren't busy enough in the 70s, I agreed to be part of a new theatrical venture aptly named the Words and Music Theater. Located on Burbank Boulevard at Sepulveda, Words and Music was the brainchild of fellow actors James Westerfield, famous for his roles as the flustered small-town police officer in such Disney classics as *The Shaggy Dog*, *The Absent Minded Professor*, and *Son of Flubber*, and Johnny Silver, who had played character roles on radio, screen, television, and stage, including the original *Guys & Dolls*.

When I was asked to direct, as well as act, I was in pig heaven. What power! Hey, theater was my first love, and getting the chance to both act and direct was a thrill that, despite everything else that was going on in my life, was sadly lacking.

The flop sweats and money troubles might have been gone, but I was quickly falling victim to the fact that a man's life rarely goes in the direction on which he had planned. Don't get me wrong. The 70s were a successful, happy, and joyous time in my life. My kids were growing up and getting to know their old man, and vice versa. Toby had never been happier, and I'd never been happier *for* her.

But in the quiet moments that came before dawn, I knew that this was not the direction I'd seen for myself. It was not the life I wanted. It's hard to fathom, the fan mail, the makeup, the wardrobe, the love scenes, the fake champagne, the bright lights, the rankings, the awards, the works, and still being dissatisfied.

But every working man reaches a point where they are on the threshold of two lives: The life they have, and the life they want. Broadway had been a pure joy, but there was never enough work to turn the joy into a career. Hollywood was a land in which you truly had to be careful what you wished for.

I'd wished for steady work … and found it. Now I was trapped by the responsibility of a wife and kids, which naturally made my choices limited. How much longer could Toby put up with my rambling ways? My wanderlust? My professional dissatisfaction? Here I was, making good money, working, living the dream of many an out of work actor, and still the big screen eluded me.

I joked that, as a soap star, I had the best of both worlds. I could still walk down the street without fear. I could still do my own grocery shopping. Could still go out in public without being mobbed. But secretly, a part of me wanted to be afraid of getting mobbed when I walked down the street. I enjoyed signing autographs in the drug store, on the street, but I could have signed *more*.

Lots more …

I don't feel that way anymore. I'm satisfied with where my life has brought me. I'm proud of what I've done. I've made peace with my career. But I can't deny that, at a certain point in my life, there was nothing I really liked about the way my career was headed. Despite the fact that, by all accounts, I was making all the right moves.

If the 70s had a personal theme song for me, it was "Hurry up and wait…"

Then along came Words and Music, and my love of the theater was renewed. It was a small theater, with only ninety-nine seats. All such theaters are ninety-nine seats, and for good reason. Under 100 chairs and you are qualified as an "equity-waiver" theater. Doesn't sound too fancy, but it's a must for the survival of smaller theaters everywhere. Equity waiver means that you can not only hire, but pay, non-equity actors.

Not that we had much to pay anybody anyway. We had a budget of $100 per performance, and that meant everybody did everything. Every night. I couldn't help but feel I was back at Bucks County Playhouse or maybe even Theater Go-Round as I schlepped around the empty theater in my shirtsleeves, hoisting curtains and toting props and building sets. If *Days* paid the bills, Words and Music made me smile.

No small feat, that …

We did several plays our first year with an open box office, among them *Bells Are Ringing, A Funny Thing Happened on the Way to the Forum*, and *Subways Are for Sleeping*. One of my favorites, though, was *Apple Tree*, a musical comedy with music by Jerry Bock and lyrics by Sheldon Harnick. A play in three acts, the first part was called "Eden," the second was "Tiger at the Gates," the third was "Cinderella," all played by the same actors.

It was the perfect 70s play. A little funny. A little out there. A little smart. A lot of laughs. You could walk away feeling like you'd had a little culture, but still laugh about your favorite scenes and hum your favorite tunes over beers later.

Now all we needed was the perfect actress …

As director of *Apple Tree*, not to mention actor, choreographer, singer, dancer, best boy, gaffer, etc., the casting of the play fell to me. Of all those who auditioned, however, a vivacious blonde named Loretta Swit was perfect for the part.

Like me, Loretta was making the rounds of all the popular TV shows of that era, doing guest performances that became standouts in such series as *Gunsmoke, Mission: Impossible* and *Mannix*.

She got the part and, I like to think, it opened doors for her. Words and Music was a popular local theater, in a town starved for live entertainment. Hollywood wasn't like Broadway, where there was a theater every two feet. Tinsel Town was a land of tape and television, and everybody from John Candor, Fred Ebb, the authors of *Caberet*, to Chita Rivera flocked to our little ninety-nine seat theater to get their live performance fix.

One of the nicest pats on the back I ever got was when Candor and Ebb said the "Lady and the Tiger" segment in *Apple Tree* was directed the best they'd ever seen. For those that don't know, it's three plays in one show, performed by the same three actors in each play doing different roles.

Not long after her star turn in *Apple Tree*, Loretta moved on to greener pastures. Army green, that is, playing the role of Major Margaret "Hot Lips" Houlihan in the TV version of the 1970 film hit *M*A*S*H*.

Guess the apple didn't fall far from that tree …

The Comedienne

Toby and I were of a new breed of modern couple, both of us working, both of us equally devoted to our three beautiful boys, both of us filling every waking moment with life, love, and laughter. Rent-a-Yenta was going strong as the 1970s played themselves out, but Toby's patience was growing thin with the escalating demands of her growing customer base.

Finding rabbis and jumping out of cakes for Hollywood's elite was one thing, but there was a limit to just how much two yentas could do. Still, the town was abuzz with this wonderful new service and Rent-a-Yenta soon hit the airwaves as the local press caught on. Toby and Lila were featured on several morning talk shows in the California market, though the two business partners went about their television appearances as differently as Christmas is to Hanukkah.

Despite the fact that Toby was a born comedienne, she did get stage fright, which she fought with a self-prescription that has been the downfall of many a performer: Shots of vodka. Luckily for her, Toby's career as a live performer was short-lived, and she stopped the vodka. Meanwhile, Lila was desperate to grab the limelight and thoroughly enjoyed the media attention. Where Toby loved it, too, Lila decided to become a stand-up comic.

For once, I enjoyed being in the audience …

In the early 80s Rent-a-Yenta soon grew too big too fast, and both women eventually tired of the rigorous demands of what had started out as just a hobby. But first, there was time for one last joke.

As Toby told it, she arrived at another pampered California housewife's backyard only to be showed a flawless, crystal blue swimming pool. "I'm going to drain this and have you paint something on the bottom," said the housewife.

"Well," hedged Toby, wondering where in the hell she was going to find someone to paint an entire pool for this woman, "what would you like painted down there?"

"I'd like a big pair of eyes wearing glasses," said the woman, quickly adding the explanation that "…my husband's an ophthalmologist."

Without blinking my wife the comedienne blurted, "Good thing he's not a gynecologist!"

As the housewife roared with laughter, it was a fitting end to a wild, bumpy ride …

Thursday's Game

Not every movie I did in the 1970s wound up on the silver screen, but there was one theme running through each and every one of them: Lasting friendships. 1974 found me on the set of a MOW, or Movie of the Week, written by small screen heavyweight James L. Brooks and directed by Robert Moore entitled *Thursday's Game*.

The premise was simple: "Harry Evers and Marvin Ellison have been playing poker Thursday nights with their friends for years. When a disagreement breaks up the game, they decide to continue meeting and doing different things together, instead of staying home with their wives. When the wives find out that the games stopped some time ago, they are a quite upset. Just what have they been doing on Thursday nights…"

The cast was anything but: Ellen Burstyn, Cloris Leachman, Valerie Harper, Rob Reiner, and, of course, yours truly, to name just a few. But the movie was built around the relationship of stars Gene Wilder and Bob Newhart.

It was a little like the *Odd Couple*, but with both of these Hollywood heavyweights playing against type. Gene Wilder was the nebbish, quiet Harry Evers and Bob was the crazy, frantic Marvin Ellison.

Both men were stars in my book, however, and never had I been on a set with less ego … and more charm. There was "no show, no blow" with these two men, who I've simply adored ever since. Here we were, a cast of men playing poker every Thursday night, and on the final day of shooting how did we choose to wrap our humble little film? With strippers, beer, and broads?

Hardly; try a massive pillow fight instead …

Jed Allan

An offshoot of my new friendship with Bob was a new friendship with his close buddy, Don Rickles. Two very funny men who couldn't have been nicer once they walked offstage. It just so happened that, while I was doing *Days*, Don was doing his show, *Ensign O'Toole*, at an NBC studio right next door. There was no greater joy than watching each other's shows while on break from our own.

Just another *Days* perk.

And still there was more to come …

Perks

Days of Our Lives took me places I never thought I could go, and some places I never even knew I'd *want* to go. *Hollywood Squares* was one, and though my stint was brief my friendship with host Peter Marshall remains strong to this day.

The guest spots, the talk shows, the MOWs, and appearances that came post-1974 I believe all were a result, to some degree, of my visibility on *Days*, but not all of the perks were professional.

Some were simply for pleasure …

In 1976 Toby and I took our first trip to Europe. It was the trip of a lifetime, not only for the destination, but for the baggage we didn't pack: Namely Mitch, Dean, and Rick. Not that we wouldn't have loved to bring them along, but that wouldn't have been much of a vacation—for *anybody*.

Instead, we invited my mother to stay at our house and treat herself to her grandchildren …

Toby and I fell in love all over again, holding hands through London, Rome, and Paris like young lovers on a second honeymoon. It was strange to see how far *Days* reached across the continents, for even in secluded nightspots or hotel lobbies I was spotted and recognized.

Halfway through our two-week jaunt, however, I got a call from our thirteen-year-old, Dean. "Dad?" he asked, the sound of trepidation, and not a little warning, in his squeaking voice.

"Yes, Deano," I answered before asking, "What's up?"

"When are you coming home?" he wanted to know.

I couldn't help but chuckle. All of our boys did everything but kick us out the door when they'd heard their beloved grandmother was coming to stay with them for two weeks. Now it seemed the shoe was on the other foot. "Why?" I chuckled.

To which Dean deadpanned, "Because you won't have a mother in a week. I swear, Dad. We can't take it. We'll poison her. I promise …"

Luckily, as dramatic as our three guys could be, they weren't very good on follow-through. Toby and I stayed the extra week and, when we got home, nobody was worse for the wear.

Though it was a few years before we took another vacation without the boys …

McMillan and Me

Hollywood is a town that looks big, but acts small. Meaning, you can't go too far without running into a familiar face, for better or worse. Most of the time it's for worse, but occasionally it can be for the better.

Sometimes, it's even for the best …

Such was the case when I watched Rock Hudson decide to try TV with a new series, *McMillan and Wife*, in the late 1970s. Hudson played San Francisco Police Commissioner Stewart McMillan, a man fortunate enough to have a wife who was both beautiful and brilliant.

As the 70s wore inevitably onward and my professional cache grew by degrees, I didn't always have time to tune in and see what Rock was doing on the show, but his presence on a highly rated weekly series gave me the hope that we would one day work together again.

The chance came in the late 70s when I appeared in Episode 39 of *McMillan and Wife*, entitled "Affair of the Heart," on March 20, 1977. I played a character named Alan Evans and was thrilled to be working with the likes of Stephanie Powers as Deputy D.A. Stephanie Bryant, and Larry Hagman as Dr. Wesley Corman.

But the real thrill was working with Rock again. It was clear that I wasn't the only one. By now the film legend turned TV icon had been in the business for decades, and it showed. On screen and off, his humility and sincerity hadn't dimmed one iota.

There are few class acts in this business.

Rock Hudson was at the top of that short list …

Curtain Call

Little did I know it, but my days at Words and Music were coming to a denouement as well. In the spring of 1977 friend and colleague James Westerfield suffered a massive stroke that left him unable to walk, let alone act.

The news came as a shock to me personally, not to mention professionally. To be cut down in his prime like that, to have that which he cherished so much—the stage, the arts, the craft, the plays—taken from him when he was just achieving such creative and artistic freedom with Words and Music was a true tragedy, and not just for James. We would all miss his warmth and humor, his passion and guidance. We were still in rehearsals for *Apple Tree* at the time, and I'll never forget the day an assistant wheeled James Westerfield into the small theater unannounced.

Though it had only been weeks since his stroke, already the formerly robust and occasionally caustic Westerfield looked like half the man he used to be. It was all I could do to keep a smiling face as I watched this formerly dynamic and talented gentleman be wheeled into the theater, helpless, his limbs foreign to him, his tongue a stranger in his own mouth.

Somehow, however, our dear friend James managed to impart his request that day. He wanted Loretta and me to sing him the songs from *Apple Tree*. Actor and actress exchanged surprised glances and, of course, eagerly complied. We just wanted to make him happy.

We sang the entire musical, a capella and unprepared, but as beautifully as we could manage on such short notice. There we were, at four in the afternoon, singing our hearts out to an audience of one, and getting the reviews of a lifetime.

From his wheelchair, Loretta and I both heard this once vibrant and powerful man weeping with emotion, joy, and gratitude. He was where he belonged, in the middle of a darkened theater enjoying a live performance and, unable to applaud, he was cheering the only way he knew how: With tears and a crooked smile.

I will never forget the unspoken gratitude of that crystal clear performance. I have performed for packed houses and rough crowds, adoring fans and stubborn hecklers, but never has a musical been met with such a powerful combination of heartbreaking sadness and uplifting inspiration.

Unfortunately, there was no chance for a repeat performance.

James Westerfield died a short month after our impromptu musical …

The Blind Leading the Blind

Like cop shows, talk shows were all the rage as the 1970s wound down. *The Mike Douglas Show*, in particular, was very receptive to soap stars such as myself and as such I was a frequent guest in the late 70s.

Mike Douglas was a sweet, dear man and a terrific talk show host. A particularly wonderful former guest was actor-singer Tom Sullivan. Tom has been around forever, it seems, although he's not that old and has never let the fact that he's been blind since birth stand in his way. Born in Boston in 1947, Sullivan was on a roll in the late 70s, starring in such feature films as *Airport '77, Love's Dark Ride* and *Cocaine Cowboys*.

His work continued on through the 80s and 90s, with guest appearances on such hit TV shows as *Fame, Knight Rider, Highway to Heaven, Designing Women, Beverly Hills, 90210,* and *Touched by an Angel.* Most recently he served as technical consultant on the 2003 Ben Affleck blockbuster *Daredevil,* in which the actor plays a blind superhero.

I remember going to his house one time before the show in question and he decided he wanted to take us horseback riding. We all got on horses, waiting for the wrangler, who took care of his horses, to take us out. The wrangler was Tom himself. Now you talk about the blind leading the blind. We actually trotted two miles through bush and forest in back of where Tom lived, following a man who couldn't see.

I don't know who had more guts, him or us …

Back to Mike Douglas. Tom was just another one of the guys, making his rounds on the talk show circuit and, on this day, taking Mike Douglas up on an improvised game of basketball – on the air. They moved a basket in because Tom said he could play and, being blind, everyone thought it would be fun to watch.

Only trouble was, Tom was so good at foul shooting that you almost forgot that he was blind. Swish after swish, Mike would retrieve the ball and zip it back over to Sullivan, hitting him in the head, the crotch, the knees, anywhere and everywhere. Bewildered, Mike would shoot me a look like, "What's wrong with this guy?"

"Hey Mike," I answered, "give the guy a break, he's blind!"

Mike got so embarrassed, so flustered, he eventually threw the ball, hard, and straight at *me*. I ducked and the ball hit the stage manager.

My last line of the interview was, "Hey Mike, that was fun, can Tom and I come back again? Maybe we can play football next time ..."

It was the only time I ever saw the talk show host speechless ...

The 80s:
From Stage to Santa Barbara

The 70s had ended on a roll and now the 80s swooped in with little transition. I was still doing *Days* and loving every minute of it, still freelancing as often as I could, burning the candle at both ends, and reaping the profits as my family soon grew more comfortable with "the actor's life."

But not everyone in the family was as comfortable as the rest ...

Our beautiful Dean was becoming a real pain in the ass. I don't know what happened, but seemingly overnight Toby and I thought we had a new kid in the house. I mean, he had always been independent, but never in trouble. The never turned to always, and suddenly we had our hands full.

I hadn't always been patient, but neither was the law. No record or "sheet," as they say, but you name it, Dean did it. The day he turned eighteen, my hair turned gray. But just like that, it seemed, he suddenly announced: "Mom, Dad, it's all over. I've turned over a new leaf, you won't have anymore trouble."

And we didn't! He's now a lawyer and a partner in his firm, gave us two beautiful grandchildren, Alexis and Nick, and is equal to his brothers in being the best father I know.

Speaking of fathers, I was weeks away from working with the man many in this business, not to mention the world, consider the "father of television comedy." Though some of you might recognize him best as an "uncle…"

Please, Spell the Name Right

Guys and Dolls and … Uncle Miltie?

You would think that having a starring role on one of television's most popular soap operas would give a guy a little confidence, but not so when an actor has become a little "rusty" in one particular area of his repertoire: In this case, it was my "pipes" that were rusty.

One day in 1984 I got a call from my manager, Arlene Dayton, asking me if I wanted to audition for the coveted part of "Sky" in a new version of *Guys and Dolls*, starring Milton Berle … and—hopefully—me.

One of the most popular and prolific Broadway musicals of the 1950s, *Guys and Dolls* was scored by composer and lyricist Frank Loesser and based on a short story by Damon Runyon entitled "The Idyll of Miss Sarah Brown."

The musical revolves around legendary character "Nathan Detroit," the mastermind behind the longest running "permanent" craps game in New York city, who bets fellow gambler Sky Masterson that he can't convince "the next girl he sees" to fall madly in love with him.

As fate would have it, the very next girl Sky lays his eyes on just happens to be Miss Sarah Brown, a notoriously kindhearted do-gooder with an aversion to gambling and most other sins, and thus the die is cast for a comedy of errors set to some of the most memorable song and dance this side of live theater.

To play one of Broadway's most memorable parts would be a thrill, but the play, the part, the music, and the lyrics all paled in comparison to the man, the legend, who was signed to play Nathan Detroit, none other than "Mister Television" himself: Legendary Milton Berle.

Born "Mendel Berlinger" on July 12, 1908, Milton began performing by the time he was only five-years-old. From stage to radio to television to the big screen, "Uncle Miltie" had done it all.

And, more often than not, done it better than everyone else …

The Milton Berle Show had been a staple in my house from the very beginning, and by the time I was tapped to audition for Sky in 1984, Milton had been a legend for decades and there was no way I could pass the opportunity to work alongside him.

Though I almost did …

Jed Allan

Stage Fright: Revisited

Instead of leaping at the chance to play Sky, like any marginally sane actor would have, I instead told my manager that "I couldn't do it." Whether I was just scared because I hadn't sung since we closed the doors at Words and Music, I wasn't sure, but I'm certain it played a large part in saying "no" to what must have obviously sounded to my manager like a "slam dunk."

Naturally, Toby got all over me when she heard the news. "Jed, honey," she insisted in her own, inimitable fashion of gentle, albeit persistent, positive reinforcement, "of course you can do it. It's like riding a bike; you never forget how. Just do some voice work for a few days before your audition. You'll see: Your voice will be back in working order in no time …"

I told her, "Honey, I'd need a few years before I got my voice back in shape, let alone a few days…"

That was the end of it. Or so I thought. Instead, Toby prodded me for two straight days until I finally agreed to get a vocal coach for the rest of the week. It was less of a crash course and more of a status report, intended to see just where I was, vocally.

Though I still felt unsure, Toby and my coach were convinced I could do it and so I eventually auditioned and, to my absolute utter disbelief, I got it! But the inner turmoil still wasn't over: Even though I had gotten the part, I was still so scared to get back on stage after such a long hiatus from live theater that I almost turned it down!

Almost …

But luckily my better half got the *better* of me: "Almost sixteen weeks in LA and San Francisco?" Toby asked in a tone that let it be known that this was in no way a question. "You don't turn that down…"

So, I didn't. I took the part, met the legend, was bowled over by his grace and charm, and took to the task of learning a new role with fever and verve. We were rehearsing, and set to open, at the famed Ahmanson Theatre.

Located in downtown Los Angeles at 135 North Grand Avenue at Temple Street, just off Hollywood Parkway and the 110, the Ahmanson is home to the Center Theatre Group, widely recognized as one of the nation's leading regional theatre companies.

So now I was on the stage, but still far from being out of the woods. And after four long weeks of rehearsing right down the hall from Robert Goulet, who was belting out tune after tune in preparation for his anticipated run in *Brigadoon*, my already shaky confidence was crumbling once again.

Listening to Goulet's effortless voice sing from one soundstage over was like rubbing salt in the wounds, and every day of rehearsals was like a battle as I struggled to blow the rust out of my pipes and try to grapple with my sudden insecurity at the same time.

However, being in that theater, playing such a wonderful part, doing live theater so close to home, doing that particular show, and co-starring with Milton Berle, come opening night the experience was truly a joy to remember, even though I thought for certain I'd never get there. We opened at the Ahmanson Theater to lovely reviews.

I don't want to blow my horn too loudly, however, because on that fateful opening night I lost the backbeat for sixteen bars on "Luck, Be a Lady" and almost didn't find my way back.

Of course Dan Sullivan, the ever observant *LA Times* reviewer caught it, but said "…except for a hairy moment during 'Lady,' Jed Allan has lovely pipes and made a wonderful Sky."

Guess they weren't so rusty after all …

Headed for a Breakdown

The rush of great reviews and live theater notwithstanding, my schedule was at an all-time frantic pace as the summer of 1980 dawned hot and hazy in sunny California. Stage performances six nights a week, and three to four full "days" on the set of *Days*?

Talk about a schedule …

It got to the point where time was most definitely *not* on my side. Instead, the clock became my greatest enemy. Getting to the Ahmanson Theater in LA wasn't so bad, but making curtain call in San Francisco? Now how do I work *that* out?

I almost didn't …

Looking back I can write this all with a steady hand, but at the time I was stressed to the max, juggling my "day job" on *Days* and renewing my love for the theater at the same time. It was enough to send a guy to the hospital.

And it did ...

One day I felt dizzy and sweaty on the set. It was something I hadn't experienced before but, at my age, knew to take the signs very seriously: It was very similar to what one might feel during a hear attack.

My friend John Clark, aka "Mickey Horton" from the show took me across the street to St. Joseph's Hospital. The diagnosis was as slim as the examination, and after a few hours the doctors said to "be careful," that "something doesn't look right."

Unsatisfied, I went to my doctor and said I had to go back to the show.

Not surprisingly, he said "You can't go back."

"I have to go back," I insisted, "my understudy isn't strong enough."

Knowing that cold hard facts would be the only way to shut me up, my doctor did a treadmill test, which proved him right. Then he recommended a cardiologist at St. Joseph's Hospital who three days later performed an angiogram. When it was over he said, "I've got good news and bad news. You've got a little problem, but not in a major area. We can treat this with medicine. Let's take it one day at a time ..."

I was happy, at least, that I listened to my own doctor and that between he and the cardiologist we caught something that could be reversed. I was only forty-three years old at the time. So much for rushing back to the play: It took me four days before I finally got to San Francisco.

And Milton didn't even ask where I'd been.

So much for a weak understudy ...

"Members" Only

As for old Milt, he was of course wonderful, crazy, annoying, lovable, helpful, selfish, giving Milton. I know that sounds strange, but he was all those things to me and the cast. He was my friend and I was his Sky. I loved him. He was sweet and caring with me, and if you can believe it, he often asked ME what I thought about HIS work!

To some of the others in the cast he was a bully, always somehow apologizing after a put-down, but I'll never forget the way he gave me the funniest line I ever heard when I tried to do a number on him one day when neither of us had anything better to do.

To all of you who don't know it already, Milton was a major womanizer, reputed to have one of, if not *the*, largest male organs in all of Hollywood. He was quite the swinger in his day, literally, and his running gag was to have a match as to who was bigger, himself or some cocky stage hand who had at one time or another bragged about the size of his own penis.

Milton would always say, "I'll take out just enough to beat him."

Eager to play a prank on the master of all pranksters, one matinee day between shows I walked into his dressing room and said, "Milton, I bet you've been bullshitting for years about the size of your dick. I bet it's a B, B- at best."

"Hey, Jed," he answered without skipping a beat. "Whenever I get an erection, I black out."

Needless to say, I was rolling on the floor, practically peeing from laughter. What a character. For years after that he'd greet me whenever we met, "Hey, Sky, how are you?"

Unfortunately, that's what he'd do during the bows at *Guys and Dolls*, introduce everyone by their cast names. The cast got in an uproar about not being properly recognized and asked me to speak to him, which I did. Whether he forgot their names or just didn't care, I never found out. But working with Milton for those sixteen weeks was a career in itself.

It's All in the Eye of the Beholder

During the early 80s I was in my prime. I had a charming character on *Days*, rubbed shoulders with TV legends onstage, and was in the terminology of the day an altogether "hot shot leading man." (Please don't think it's bragging, but you'll see why I mention all of this in a second.)

One night during the early 80s, Toby and I went to see a performance of *South Pacific* starring Howard Keel and Jane Powell at the famed Pantages Theater in Hollywood.

Now, it's true that actors don't watch shows the same way "civilians" do, and I suppose I'm no different, for as I was watching the play that evening I noticed an old dancer I knew from *All-American* in the 60s named Tony Falco.

Here was Tony, still doing chorus work, some twenty-one years later. It really bothered me, I felt so bad for him. I mentioned it to Toby, pointed him out, and said, "What a shame, honey, twenty-five years gone by and he's still doing chorus work."

Here I've been pretty successful for all these years, doing *Days* and all these other TV shows, movies of the week, film, *Guys and Dolls*, and yet here was Tony still struggling in the trenches.

As luck would have it, they were having a party backstage after the performance and Toby and I were invited. Seeing Tony, I walked up and said a few warm words to him.

"Tony," I said, "how are you doing? You look great, it's so good to see you again …"

Tony looked back and gave a big "Hello."

Then he said something that put all of my "success" right back into perspective. "I'm great, Jed," says the chorus dancer. "How about you? Are you still in the business?"

"It's all in the eyes of the beholder …"

I guess he didn't own a TV …

Country & Beyond

Nashville. Oh how I love that town. During the early 80s when I was really hot on *Days of Our Lives*, I was often invited to Nashville either to do *Nashville Now* with legendary host and all-around country celebrity Ralph Emery as guest host or, in a gig that was just as fun: As a replacement and/or co-host for the local NBC station, WSM-TV.

Nashville Now was great, a rip-roaring, good-time show that featured such other fine guests as Annette Funicello, Davy Jones, and The Monkees. And hosting TV? That just brought me back to my days of live television with a magical sense of nostalgia.

But the best thing to happen during my Nashville nocturne was getting to meet the cast of *Hee Haw* and, better yet, being invited to do the show on several different occasions.

Please, Spell the Name Right

Roy Clark. Buck Owens. And George Lindsey, my neighbor and friend from Broadway's *All-American*. (Though you might remember him best as "Goober" from *Mayberry RFD*.) Lindsey and I were actually neighbors at the time. He lived in Tarzana back then, which was about a mile away from me and Toby. His son George, Jr. and my son Mitch even became friends of sorts.

Small world, isn't it?

Or was it luck? Either way, my days in Nashville were full of it.

And, speaking of luck:

Gloom, despair, and agony on me! (WOE!)
Deep, dark depression, excessive misery! (WOE!)
If it weren't for bad luck, I'd have no luck at all. (WOE!)
Gloom, despair, and agony on me!

Few can forget the lyrical refrain from one of the most popular TV series of the 70s, the "Woe is Me" song from that lovable classic, *Hee Haw*. *Hee Haw* (it's working title was "Country Corn") actually got its start as a weekly series in 1969 on CBS.

Despite its immediate popularity, however—some called it the "redneck version" of Rowan & Martin's *Laugh-In*—the network canceled it in 1971 as part of an attempt to distance itself from the "rural flavor" of other popular hits canceled that same year, including TV icons *The Beverly Hillbillies* and *Green Acres*. (The show was later revived and lived on for another twenty some years.)

The show's slapstick jokes might have kept them rolling in the aisles, but the music kept steadily growing audiences—including myself—coming back week after week. Loyal viewers, and even first-timers, could expect to see two or three country music stars, including Hank Williams, Jr., Johnny Cash, Dolly Parton, Tammy Wynette, Loretta Lynn, and Willie Nelson, and even some notable up and comers, including such "youngins" as George Strait, Alan Jackson, Travis Tritt, and Vince Gill perform live each week.

Sometimes, they also participated in the lively skits that loyal fans grew to know and love. These included Pickin & Grinnin, Archie's Barbershop,

Jed Allan

Empty Arms Hotel, KORN Radio, Lulu's Truck Stop, Minnie's School, and everyone's favorite: The Cornfield Jokes.

I was one of those stars lucky enough to guest on *Hee Haw* from time to time, but the connection went much deeper than that. The show's friendly, unassuming, and talented hosts, Buck Owens and Roy Clark, soon became wonderful friends, and I immediately felt right at home in Nashville where, thanks to my current success on *Days of Our Lives*, I was welcomed with open arms.

So much so that, for a time, Nashville became something of a second home to Toby and me. Hanging around all the country people, meeting everyone we'd enjoyed watching on TV for years, it was all a thrill.

And you heard it here first: Those country folk? They sure know how to party. The Oakridge Boys. The Statler Brothers. Larry, Steve, and Rudy Gatlin of the Gatlin Brothers. Talk about wild guys.

Here I was, Mr. Big City Guy, trying to keep up with these "hicks" and it wasn't even a possibility. Through the years that followed, we'd run into each other all over the country doing benefits and charity events. Those were truly a great couple of years in my career.

Hee Haw was, without a doubt, the most fun I ever had working on any TV show. Being in a cornfield surrounded by those beautiful, buxom *Hee Haw* "Honeys," like Linda Thompson, once married to Elvis Presley, and still a knockout at the time, trading barbs with the Hagar brothers, singing with Minnie Pearl and the gang. What could be better? Why, Kenny Rogers even found his third wife in the cornfields of *Hee Haw*.

I sang several times on the show, right at home in a barnyard setting while sitting on a bale of hay with all those lovely *Hee Haw* Honeys surrounding me. Talk about a lot of fun.

And then, "Along Came Jones."

Or whatever his name was.

He was a *Hee Haw Nashville Now* Opryland groupie. About fifty-years-old, "Jones" always traveled with his wife, or who we assumed was his wife. Everybody knew him, or thought they did. Better yet, for him anyway, we all accepted him; invited him to parties, golf trips, benefits.

He looked like he belonged.

Please, Spell the Name Right

What did we know?

He befriended everyone he met and never mentioned or talked about what he did for a living. We all assumed he was loaded, since he was the big "wine buyer," as they say, picking up checks for everything. Dinners, taxis, limousines, you name it. He was the original "Mr. Nice Guy." The Sweetheart of Sigma-Chi.

He was also the biggest con man any of us had ever met.

It started off slowly enough, as he calculatedly began ingratiating himself with everybody. Getting to be everybody's friend, mentioning deals everywhere, dropping clues, hints, sniffing around. And always willing to trade a little "insider information," if you know what I mean.

If anyone was interested, that is.

Sadly, most of us were …

He was the original cool customer, spreading his cash around and making a good impression, and always playing it very slow. Very cool. He always made sure someone overheard about one of his deals, and was careful never to look as if he had brought up the subject himself.

Then came the oil wells. By now we'd heard about this deal and that, and little by little he was getting everybody interested in all these oil wells he supposedly owned, most of them in Lubbock, Texas.

In addition to his many other talents, which as far as I could tell involved flagging down taxis, ordering wine, and spreading around big tips, he was apparently also a wildcatter drilling for oil and, out of the goodness of his own heart, was willing to sell shares to anyone interested.

Amazingly, dozens of us took him up, including many of the cast and crew, George Lindsey, myself, and about seven of my relatives. I would say, all told, he must have picked up a quarter of a million dollars in "investments."

One of the highlights—if you could call it that—of this whole ordeal was that, after I paid him my money, I remarked casually to him, more as an offhand joke: "When do I see my well?"

Without batting an eyelash he said, "I'll have your ticket ready for Lubbock anytime you want it." So about a month later he and I go down to Lubbock, Texas. We got there at 7 or 8 o' clock at night, checked into the hotel, and, by the time we get to the wells themselves it's about ten p.m. so they're all lit up.

Out of a row of gleaming, pumping, spewing oil wells he points to one well in particular and says, "That's yours."

I said, "You're kidding."

He said, "No, take a walk around and I'll take your picture." So I hugged the well, and he took a picture. (What I wouldn't give for *that* snapshot today!) And I thought, "I'm an oil owner." I was just like a kid in a candy store. Here we were, all these wells around me, lit up like some movie set, making somebody money.

And now they were going to be making *me* money.

JR, look out …

Okay, fade out, fade in. I go back to LA, I wait for some checks to start showing up and begin lining my coffers. He says you'll be getting some "big checks" soon. Soon, maybe. Big? Hardly. Fact was, my first check was for ten and a half dollars; my next check was for *four* dollars.

And my family? Their checks were nada, zip, nothing. I finally tried to complain to him but, not surprisingly, no one could get a hold of him. He'd disappeared off the face of the earth. Everyone else from *Hee Haw* wanted to know where he was, too, but by now he was nowhere to be found.

He was smart, though. I'll give him that. No one lost enough money to kill themselves over. Instead, he did it in chunks. Nuggets. Bite size morsels. A little here. A little there. You're in for how much? And what about *you*?

Over time, however, and with enough people "investing," it sure added up. I lost fifteen grand, my family all told lost twenty-five grand, and don't think they ever let me forget about it, either. I ended up paying my father-in-law back, but the rest had to fend for themselves.

From my country family the investments spread out to my daytime family: John Clark from *Days of Our Lives* lost ten grand, too.

We later heard through the grapevine that our groupie had been arrested on some other crackpot scheme. We all remembered his original name, or at least we thought it was his name, but he was obviously using aliases so none of us could catch him on this latest charge.

So much for playing the role of filthy rich oil barren …

It was a soft lesson learned, and a scar that's still fresh. To this day, I don't even put oil in my car myself. Even with all that aggravation shrouding my time in television's most famous cornfield, however, doing *Hee Haw* was a joy and truly a great time in my career.

I formed lasting friendships with many from the show, and George Lindsey and I hung out frequently for many, many years after that. I don't see him as much as I used to anymore, but still run into him occasionally and that, I suppose, serves to soften the loss just a tad.

Oh well. As they say down in Texas, "Oil's Well That Ends Well …"

The "Days" of Ageism

Fortune, of course, has a way of evening itself out over the course of time. So it was perhaps prophetic that I ran into Tony Falco that fateful night backstage after *South Pacific*, for shortly after that meeting I'd be feeling like just another chorus member myself, and reflecting on Tony's unintentional comment on the fleeting whims of fame.

By the early 80s, the writing was on the wall for myself and a few of the other so-called "aging" regulars on *Days*. Divorced, twice, remarried, twice, with a girlfriend—this is Don Craig, of course, not Jed Allan, in case you thought I was leaving the juicier parts out of my life story—it seemed like the writers had poor old Don stuck in a holding pattern and headed out to pasture.

I'd always had a blast on the show and the people I worked with all made it a fun experience, but as the 80s dragged on so did my enthusiasm for the soap. It just wasn't as fun to go into work anymore, and maybe it was because those of us who weren't quite as limber and supple as we used to be knew our days were finally numbered.

I was still freelancing outside the show doing different things, television, movies of the week, feature films here and there, and it seemed that at long last the joy of doing *Days* was finally nearing an end.

They weren't writing much for me, and I could tell it was because of the ageism that was rampant at the time—and still is today—among those who produce shows in which youth, beauty, and certain "physical assets" are valued much more highly than are talent, class, and charm.

New characters on the top-rated daytime drama were getting younger and, if you watch soaps today, you can see predominantly young people, except for a few old timers who were there from way back, and who somehow manage to hold onto a loyal fan base who would give producers the fight of their lives were these daytime legends ever to be done away with.

The year was 1984, and I had just heard about a new show being cast called *Santa Barbara*. Feeling unappreciated and under worked at *Days*, I put a call in to the head of daytime about it. The call went to a young man named Brian Fronz who, at the time, happened to be all of thirty-six years old.

Try being a few years away from fifty, and telling a thirty-six-year-old what's "right for you." It was clear from his tone that he didn't want me, even before he said, "No you're wrong for it, you're too young…"

Of course, this last was a surprise. It was the first I'd heard about being "too young" for a part in some time now. But Brian explained that the part was for the role of a patriarch of the Capwell dynasty, head of the richest family in Santa Barbara, a medium-sized city with a population of 90,000 an hour and a half north of Los Angeles.

Naturally, being told I wasn't right for the part made me want it all the more. Now I was frothing at the mouth I wanted it so badly. But they didn't want me to leave *Days* and they didn't want to give me a shot on the new show, so there I was, as the song says, "stuck in the middle…"

It cost them plenty of time and money and ratings not to give me a shot at NBC's newest soap opera, and they lived to regret it in the long run, as I'll tell you later on.

"Please, Mr. Postman …"

Somehow I wound through 1984 in limbo, toiling away on the *Days* set and struggling with fewer lines—and even less confidence. I freelanced as often as possible, if only to test my chops and, more importantly, prepare for the inevitable, and finally 1985 dawned with not only a new year, but a new "option."

I'd missed my shot at *Santa Barbara*, as the role of CC Capwell was filled by an older, more veteran performer and apparently to much acclaim: The soap was doing quite well, according to network scuttlebutt. I didn't much care anymore, of course. Why watch the ass end of a ship that's sailing into the sunset?

The frustration with *Days* and the missed opportunity with *Santa Barbara* left me with a foul taste for soaps in my mouth, which wasn't sweetened any when my contract came up for renewal later that year.

Not only were they cutting my lines, now they wanted to cut my "guarantee"—daytime speak for salary—in half. I was enraged. Through no fault of my own, I was being docked in pay. Turns out I wasn't alone, and that year many of the older cast member's guarantee had been slashed in half like price tags on Christmas trees at a sale on December 26th.

I'd worked like a dog for that soap, coming in early, staying late. Never once had I called in sick, not even on the busiest of days when I was burning the candle at both ends with other commitments, big or small. Even a major back problem hadn't kept me from showing up on the set. And now I was being punished for being older?

Against my manager's wishes, naturally, since it would cost her a sizable chunk of dough every year, I decided to quit, not having the faintest idea of how I'd make a dollar in the months, or even years, to come.

It might have been rash, but I just couldn't stand the idea of someone giving me a gold watch and putting me out to pasture. Not when I'd worked so hard, not when I was in my prime, not when I'd invested so much in a character who was so well-loved by not only the fans, but other cast members as well.

Not *yet* …

Instead of re-upping my contract, I gave the producers my notice. "I'm leaving in a month," I said, with little fanfare and even less bullshit.

"Sure he is," they must have thought, rolling their eyes. "He's going to walk away from half of what he was making, which was still a six figure number, just a smaller six figures. Yeah, right …"

But leave I did …

They didn't believe it, that much was obvious by the lack of planning and foresight on their part, and they didn't write me out until the last week when I finally had to say to the writers, "You know guys, I'm not coming back after Monday. You knew that, right?"

Their response was a startled, "No, we didn't."

And I said, "Well, you better think of something, because I'm not coming back."

Even then, the warnings went unheeded. I'll never forget my final scene, aired on April 17, 1985 in which I was talking to yet another new young, female cast member.

I said, "I have to go do something."

She said, "Where are you going?"

I said, "I'm going to mail a letter…"

Then I walked out the door, never to return again. Apparently, the letter went out by Pony Express, but by now it was no matter: That was how my run on *Days of Our Lives* ended.

The rest of the cast, of course, were wonderfully sweet and supportive. The writers and producers did their best to show their good side. They gave me a wonderful going away party and a beautiful set of golf clubs and I was grateful to them. Not just for the party and the gift, but the wonderful opportunity they'd given me and the chapter they'd written in my eventful life.

I hated the way it happened, but they left me with little choice and, to this day, I have no regrets about my decision—or a single day I spent on the *Days* set. Susan Seaforth and Bill Hayes left shortly after I did, following suit for the very same reasons.

From Jupiter to *Santa Barbara*

Leaving my job of nearly thirteen years was as chilling as it was exhilarating. Naturally, I was concerned about my future. And I wasn't alone. Toby was of course a part of the decision, and now that the boys were old enough to understand what their old man was up to, we all had a stake in my future.

But before I had the chance to rediscover my first real case of flop sweat, thank God, I remembered that a production of *Guys and Dolls* was going to open in Florida that same month for ten weeks of performances at Burt Reynolds' popular Jupiter Theater in Jupiter, Florida.

It just so happened I knew the director, Charles Nelson Reilly, from the time he'd been a guest on the *Merv Griffin Show* when I was co-hosting with Merv. We'd exchanged numbers, because I liked him he was fun to be around and probably the best fill director I ever met, that means taking a "nothing moment" and making a *something* moment.

We got along great on the show, and now, eager not only for work but a chance to reprise my role as Sky, I called him almost immediately. "Charlie," I said after a few minutes spent catching up, "I finished *Days* and, as a matter of fact, I did Sky with Berle at the Ahmenson five years ago. Have you found anybody yet?"

Charlie was thrilled that I'd saved him the time, money, and effort of finding someone to play Sky, let alone learn the part, and so in April of 1985 I missed not a single beat from *Days* and went into a nice ten-week run at the dinner theater there in Jupiter. Not only had I eased right into the role, but I got to stay in Burt's condo, right on the beach.

Talk about landing on your feet …

Life was suddenly a joy again. There I was, back on the stage where I belonged, and reprising a role I'd learned only a few years back. Morning walks on the beach combined with appreciative Florida audiences and packed houses had me feeling good about myself again, and when the ten-week run of *Guys* was over I quickly learned of an upcoming production of *Come Blow Your Horn* over in nearby St. Petersburg.

From sunny Jupiter I traveled to sunny St. Pete and enjoyed another eight straight weeks of solid stage performances that were a soothing balm for my troubled soul. It was amazing: Just after quitting *Days* I'd managed to land eighteen straight weeks of work, all with a single phone call!

"How lucky can you get?" I thought.

I was about to find out …

I returned to our family home in California during the middle of October, 1985 and only days later received a phone call from my manager. "You're never gonna believe who wants you!" he said, answering on my behalf before I could even reply: "Santa Barbara! They want you to read for the patriarch of the show."

"Why, what happened?"

"I dunno," he mused, "I guess they're working out the kinks over there. They've been through four guys there already, pros, too. The first one, Lloyd Bochner, had a heart attack and who still might be doing it if he hadn't. And the last one was Charlie Bateman. I guess they want you to replace Charlie …"

"I can't believe this," I said. "They can't find what they want in *those* guys?"

"The ratings aren't good," was all my manager would offer. "I dunno, I don't know the whole story, and maybe *you* don't want to know …"

"Ain't that the truth," I thought, hanging up.

Beware the Soap Opera Coma

Like myself, the latest industry veteran to play *Santa Barbara* patriarch CC Capwell was an old hand at soap operas. In fact, Charlie Bateman had played Maxwell Jarvis on *Days of Our Lives* in the early 1980s.

Apparently he, too, had been the latest to suffer from ageism on the set.

Only to be burned twice after landing on *Santa Barbara* …

I felt bad about Charlie, but took the audition anyway. What else could I do? It felt strange, at first, being back on the NBC lot in Burbank, but this was the part I'd been chomping at the bit to play nearly two years earlier and it just seemed right that I go.

Besides all that, I needed a job!

It soon became quite clear, however, that the read through wasn't a command performance to honor Jed Allan. The producers were behind the eight-ball and I was informed that I'd have to test on camera with six other guys that day. This on top of the fact that they'd already seen a bunch of guys before me and could be considering any one of them at the same time.

Having been through this once or twice already, however, I knew what to expect. When auditioning for a lead on a soap, you don't just walk in with your pages and shake hands with the execs. What you do is you sign a "test contract," which basically lets you know what you're going to be earning beforehand, just in case you nail the audition and actually get the part.

Though on the surface it sounds to the uninitiated like it would be in the actor's favor, it's really only in a *starving* actor's favor. In reality, it's designed so that the producers can pay as little as they can get away with before you audition just in case they love you to death. Then they've covered their asses beforehand. At least for the first contract, which could be three years.

Usually, this is done before an actor even gets the script, but in this case I'd been sent the script—and no contract. I assumed this might mean that the offer wasn't all that serious or that, perhaps, they'd already given the part to someone and forgot to tell me about.

Trust me, stranger things had happened …

For this reason I only looked at the script peripherally, not memorizing my lines per se as I might for a "real" audition. So much about the read through seemed strange, why should memorizing the script be any different?

Come the day of the audition I still had no signed contract, and an only partially memorized script. As I suspected, they didn't want to test me until I'd signed a contract. Ten minutes before my test, a contract appeared. I signed and within half an hour I was reading across from Judith McConnell, who would eventually become my wife, Sophia, on the show.

After the test, dear Judy whispered in my ear how well I'd done, and she thought I had it, even after testing with as many men as she had that day. It was shades of my love scene with Deidre Hall all over again, only this time I was on the opposite side of the kissing booth.

So while Judith may have liked me, the producers had seen me glancing at my script on camera and were worried that I "wouldn't be able to learn my lines." This from a guy who'd just spent thirteen years showing up day in, day out on *Days of Our Lives*, "almost" never flubbing a line … well, maybe once in a while.

I understood their hesitance, though. I really did. After all, they'd just been through four veteran actors who hadn't had the chemistry they were looking for. To them, I was just another odd number who may or may not deliver the goods come game time.

Jed Allan

I could tell they were impressed up to a point, but I got the feeling something was bothering them. They just couldn't trust the audition. I left without closure, and got a phone call the following day saying that they would "let me know" in "a week or so."

The old industry standard for, "Don't call us, we'll call you …"

One week, then two, then *three* went by and through the grapevine I heard they were still looking at other people. I called my manager and told her, "I'm through. Call 'em and tell 'em the deal's off. Tell 'em I don't want the job …"

Why I made this call I had no idea. I didn't have another job and, in fact, hadn't worked in a month and a half. The last show I'd done was *Come Blow Your Horn*, which ended back in October. I just felt like I was really being pushed into a corner. "If it didn't work with these four other guys in a year and a half on the air," I thought, "they're scared to death to have to make a decision. I felt I had to make it for them …"

Stupid, maybe.

But maybe not …

California Calling

She made the call and told them how I felt. They said "He's still in there," but as I thought, they were concerned about getting it wrong again. I told her to call back, tell them I'm going to Europe for Thanksgiving, and that "the ball was in their court."

Where I got the guts to do this, I'll never know. Toby, myself, and another couple decided at the last minute to leave town and have fun instead of sitting around and waiting for the phone like I have for most of my professional life.

"If they want to get a hold of me," I told my manager, "here's the number at the hotel where I'll be staying …"

England was beautiful, the weather on Thanksgiving was gorgeous, we had an incredible time with our friends, and we were even going to stay an extra couple of days, when guess what? The phone rings in the room.

It was one of the producers asking, "Will you test again?"

I thought, "I can't believe this. Again? I don't understand it. Why? What would I possibly do in a second reading that I hadn't done in the first?" But still, the business side of me thought: They're just trying to be safe.

"Yes," I answered, but there was more.

"You can't do it with a script," he said.

Of course not, were they totally wacky? I didn't have a contract and had only gotten the script two hours before the first test. Now I had two days. I had taken the script with me, just in case.

Luckily, I had a long flight home. On the way I asked my friend to cue me, as he read Judith's lines and I read my own. After day of resting up from my jet lag, I came in and tested.

Again ...

Two days later, I got the part, and for the next seven and a half years I was CC Capwell on one of NBC's highest-ranked soap operas ever. More than that, I essentially had carte blanche as to how to play CC.

It was the greatest joy up to that point in my career. It was the greatest part you could have on a soap. I could add layer upon layer upon layer to make CC Capwell what I wanted him to be. Freedom. Freedom. Never having this much in my career I fully intended to squeeze as much life into, and out of, this wonderful role.

And, I guess it's safe to say, it worked ...

The "Real" World

Like most actors on soaps know (but Charlie Bateman might have suspected but didn't want to believe), by the time your character slips into a coma on a soap it means your pink slip could be waiting in your dressing room. He, however, had no idea he was being replaced and, apparently, the cast of silver-haired devils strolling in and out of the producer's office to read with Judith hadn't tipped him off, either.

They never told him ...

I was amazed that the show's executive producer, Mary-Ellis Bunim, who would later go on to single-handedly "invent" reality television on MTV with her wildly popular reality series *The Real World* and *Road Rules*, and who I eventually became good friends with she and her husband Bob, had never said a word to Charlie about his ensuing departure from the show.

I suppose she was too busy planning her upcoming Christmas party to which I, as *Santa Barbara*'s newest cast member, had been invited. Wanna know who else was invited? That's right: The "other" CC, Charlie Bateman.

I couldn't believe it when my old *Days* pal walked through the door and noticed me standing there at the bar, cocktail in hand, big as you please. "Hey Jed," he said casually, not having seen me since our *Days* days. "What are you doing here?"

You could have heard a pin drop as word spread through the formerly festive party like fireworks. Everyone else in that room, including myself, knew Charlie was out. The only one who didn't know, it seemed, was old Charlie. I wanted to tell him.

I didn't want to tell him.

I *had* to tell him …

"Charlie," I said after he'd gotten his drink (I figured he'd need it), "can I talk to you for a minute?"

As we walked to a quiet corner of the room I asked him, "Are you okay?"

He chuckled nervously and responded, "I was a little concerned about being in a coma, but they said it was okay and invited me to the party. So I guess that mean's everything is all right, *right?*"

I sighed, bit the bullet, and said, "Charlie, I gotta tell you—I'm here because I'm replacing you."

"You gotta be kidding," he said when he could finally speak. "You mean to tell me that rotten b—h invited me to her party knowing I was out on my ass and invited you, too?"

Then he suddenly saw Mary-Ellis, who had been markedly absent unto this point, and immediately tried to go and confront her. I grabbed him and said, "Don't Charlie, don't. Don't embarrass yourself, don't make it worse. I know it's a bitch, but don't do it. Nothing's going to change."

So he walked out the door, and I never saw him again.

Fortunately, he was going to be a wealthy man by inheritance and has since retired, quite happily I'm sure. But to be let go in such an uncaring, heartless way was truly a travesty and, to this day, me having to tell him remains one of the most odious tasks I've ever had to perform.

P. S. Ms. Bunim, sadly, recently passed away ...

CC Capwell (#5)

Santa Barbara was poised to break new ground in the genre of soap operas, which themselves had been breaking new ground ever since the 80s began. "Out of the closet," so to speak, and loving every minute of it, soaps became a country's least guilty "guilty pleasure."

As video recorders became more accessible—and less expensive—and the rise of "work at home" jobs rose with a sudden groundswell, so did the ravenous appetite of daytime viewers. In fact, by the 1980s, some fifty million American viewers "followed" one or more soap operas, including two-thirds of all women living in homes with TVs.

As ratings increased, so did budgets, and now the sets of soap operas rivaled that of feature films. In fact, such was the confidence of NBC at the time that the network had built the largest studio ever used by a daytime soap up to that point. Studio 11, where I was to spend the next seven and a half years, had cost close to twelve million dollars.

No wonder they were nervous about hiring another CC!

Charlie Bateman had made his "final exit" by December of 1985 and soon it was me lying on that hospital bed in a coma. There were a few bumps in the road during the transition, including the whitening of my hair to match Charlie's, but that lasted only a couple of weeks because it was so ridiculous looking. I looked less like a millionaire patriarch of a seaside California town and more like ... George Washington.

Slowly, as I woke from the coma, not to mention getting rid of that presidential hair, I could step into CC's shoes and create my version of the patriarch character who would rule *Santa Barbara* with an iron fist. I can honestly say it was some of the most fun I've ever had.

In those days, before they changed the system, we were up quite early in the morning. On the set by six a.m., we were often dog tired by the time taping wrapped for the day, and as more and more actors complained, the producers were forced to take notice.

By staggering the schedule, by trying new ideas, by adopting new routines, eventually we had the best of both worlds: A great job and an even better schedule. Some days we'd finish by noon, and I'd by home by two in the afternoon. Other times we'd go in late, and still be out by four. Four days a week max? Who can complain with a schedule like *that*.

But one of the best perks was the amount of time we got off. My first year I got three weeks off, and from there it only got better. My second year it was four weeks, my third year it was five, and when I topped out at six weeks off a year in my fourth season, who was I to complain?

The trips I took, the places I went, the times Toby and I had together, the hours I was able to spend with my kids, free and clear, you couldn't write your own life story better than I had it at that time.

It was just like being on a soap opera …

Growing Pains

My first year on *Santa Barbara* was as tumultuous as my winning of the part, softened only by the increase in ratings that, by the way, I take only minor credit for. I was surrounded by probably one of the greatest casts ever assembled in soaps at that time, and I was honored that I seemed to fit seamlessly.

It meant a great deal to me that I could be a part of that whirlwind rise to the top of the ratings, not to mention awards: We won thirteen of the sixteen Emmys we were nominated for my second year on the show.

The names will be familiar to loyal fans *and* those who've never heard of the show before: A Martinez, who played Cruz to perfection and later went on to even greater success in nighttime roles such as his star turn on the hit show, *Profiler*.

There was my daughter on the show, the young, talented, and gorgeous Robin Wright, who would eventually win hearts and minds with her dazzling performance in the feature film *The Princess Bride*. One heart, in particular, she won over in a *big* way: That of her husband, Sean Penn.

On *SB* I was married seven times, off and on, but the same woman I always came back to was Sofia, played by the charming and beautiful Judith McConnell, whom I still speak to often.

Another charming beauty, an extremely talented Louise Sorel, my dear friend played Augusta. She was married to Lionel, played by Nick Coster, and I wasn't alone in my obvious reverence for the show's *real* star: Dame Judith Anderson, who played Minx Lockridge, God rest her soul.

Though the old gal used cue cards later in her life, she could make a line sing like Pavarotti. Fans weren't the only ones to mourn her loss when she died of pneumonia on January 3, 1992.

The 90s:
Fame Has a New Zip Code

God, it can't be the 90s …

I just got to California a couple of years ago, didn't I? I was the father of three little boys, the husband of the greatest lady in the world, all this is still the same, but I just looked in the mirror as I'm writing this and no longer am I a man who is simply playing a patriarch … I *am* a patriarch!

"Where have all the flowers gone?"

By now the boys were men, Toby was still gorgeous, and suddenly I looked like I robbed the cradle. I'm not saying I looked bad, exactly, but she looked *great*. Only someone who smiles all the time, is happy all the time, stays young forever.

Me?

I better start smelling some more roses …

Anyway, *Santa Barbara* was still going strong. There were lots of cast changes, not as many Emmys, but we still had one hell of a show—and it was still a joy to go to work. Lane Davies, who played my elder son, left the show and was replaced by two different people, Terry Lester and Gordon Thompson, respectively. Beverly Garland's daughter, Carrington, took over for Robin Wright, and other new characters also came and went.

Some changes worked out great, others didn't, but harmony was still a key word on our show and in the artistic department especially, it was a constant. The problems we were starting to have were coming from up-stairs. We changed executive producers at least four times, maybe five, I can't really remember. A couple of them I loved, one I liked, one I tolerated, and one was really an ass.

And in on a pass …

Isn't that great poetry?

As the years go by the likes, dislikes, and tolerations change, but you take some of the good things from everybody. In daytime drama, unless you're a novice, you're pretty much on your own.

There is no time for directors to give direction, no real time to smooth out problems. Instead, you have to come prepared in all ways, being equipped emotionally being the hardest, learning your lines being the easiest.

The latter, for me, was true; for others not so true. But in those days we had cue cards, just in case, except the last two years of the show when executive producer Paul Rauch took them away. Panic set in but, to tell you the truth, we were better actors without them.

As time would tell …

Paul was an interesting character. Tough to love or like, but he knew his job and took control. We got along well and I considered him a friend, until he got more rude than usual. I have difficulty with rudeness.

I'm really sorry about that …

A couple of other producers disappointed the hell out of me several years later, especially when I called one for help after Toby passed away.

I'll get into that a little later …

The Beginning of the End

With all the uproar upstairs, the wonderful cast of Santa Barbara was plying its trade to the utmost. The show was still doing well in the ratings, but not as well as the first four years. Why we were not sure, but there was certainly nothing to worry about at this point.

Or was there?

I was now into my four weeks a year vacation situation and looked forward to taking two weeks at a time so as not to disrupt the writers too much. More than two weeks off for any one character at a time would be hellacious for the writing team.

Toby and I were traveling all over the world on our vacations. Ah, the joys of success. Australia, Europe, New Zealand, cruises to the Caribbean, cruises to the Mediterranean, cruises to Alaska. My God, what fun we were having, with more to come.

Of course, not all of our fun happened abroad. Some of it was much, *much* closer to home. One of our houses in the Hollywood Hills had so many steps, from the entrance to the house up to my bedroom I once counted seventy-five steps, and that was bypassing the den, the dining room, kitchen, and upstairs. There were so many of them that I literally had to plan my day around when I was going to change my clothes.

But the view was incredible!

Anyway, we eventually sold "The House of 75 Steps" and, after living in a hotel for fourteen months while house hunting, eventually moved into an older Mexican house in Los Angeles. The house had an apartment separated from the main house for my son Rick. He was the only one left living with us at the time.

Mitch was on his own by now. Meanwhile, Dean had gotten married to Merrill and we had Alexis, our first grandchild. She's twelve now and a joy to talk to.

Very soon to come was Mitch marrying Jamie. And then our second grandchild, a boy named Jake, was born in 1992. Another joy for Toby and me. He's eleven now, a child with incredible soul.

The little Mexican house was in a perfectly convenient area in LA, and we enjoyed the hell out of it. Parties, friends, relatives all the time. Life was wonderful, but soon, very soon, not to be so wonderful.

Just Biding Her Time …

Life on the set of *Santa Barbara* was busy, and most of the time I loved being there. There was an exception: Rauch was producer then and hired a young lady to replace a cast member. And this lady was to be a May – December romance for yours truly.

However, for the three months she was there, this person made my life a living hell. As an actor, of course, you have to put your feelings aside and persevere, no matter what. But this girl was about the angriest young person I'd ever met. From the minute she'd walk on stage in the morning she was pure torture to us all. Crew and cast alike, there was almost never a kind word or smile for anyone.

She was a beautiful girl, but had such deep-seated anger in her that it showed on her face in every line she read. Even if it was a light, loose scene.

"Why'd you take the role?" I once asked her.

Her response? "I'm killing time until something better comes along."

She almost killed *me* …

What a drag she was, and how hard she made it for herself and everyone around her. She was living with one of the nicest guys, and one of the most well-known actors of the time, and no one could figure out why. Mentioning names would only hurt him, and that I don't want to do.

She finally left after three months of torturing everybody, and there was no going away party. Only two times in my career did I have this occur. I mean, we all have things we personally deal with every day of our lives, but as actors you can't bring your baggage with you.

It catches up to you some day.

Even if you're too young to have packed much …

The Writing's On the Wall

Back to the show, or should I say, "No show?"

In late 1992, the writing was on the wall for the demise of *Santa Barbara*. The infighting, the lawsuits, the personality clashes, and the changes upstairs did not bode well and feedback was coming down that we had about six months left. No one panicked, exactly, but we were certainly concerned.

We loved the show and wanted it to run forever …

The thought of closing down *Santa Barbara* was anathema to us. Every week for the next six months, we'd hear new rumors about "maybe yes," "maybe no," "maybe maybe." Then, in January of 1993 it finally happened, we were given notice that we were "gone in four weeks!"

Before all this bad news even started, however, Toby and I were spending money like a smart actor should never do. Toby got on me, saying, "Save it honey; let's have some left for the bad times."

I kept thinking there would never be anymore bad times …

The Mexican house was costing me a fortune, and we bought a second house in Lake Arrowhead, not to mention building a house on the beach in Oxnard! In 1990 I sold my first little wonderful beach house, called Windy Gables, also in Oxnard. It was once owned by Clark Gable and Carole Lombard in 1939. Their little getaway became ours, and was worth a lot due to the 1985–1990 real estate boon.

So we sold it in 1990, made a lot of money, and stupidly put it into a lot on *another* beach where we were building our "dream house." How dumb can one actor get? So now I've got the Mex house, Lake Arrowhead, and on top of it all have started building the beach house. And now I find in one month I'm out of work.

Major salary to zero overnight. But did I panic?

You bet your ass I did …

House Hunting

I'm paying three mortgages, what do I do now? In my heart and soul, I thought someone would call me for another soap in a month or two, I really did.

I was CC Capwell, patriarch to the world. Everybody would want me. Oh really? One, two, three months went by—and nothing. The panic was starting to set in, and there was lots and lots of flop sweat like in the early days of coming to LA. I never thought it would happen again.

And suddenly I'm right back where I started from …

Who do I pay today? What should I do about the Mex house? How about Lake Arrowhead? The beach house was still eating me up, though it was nearly finished. One thing I didn't mention, though it was a good idea at the time, my good friends Bernie and Nicole Katz owned a lot on the beach, also.

So when we decided to build we deeded to each other half of the other's lots and so we were partnered with each other in the lot we were building on. So the losses were half as much, though in the long run it was a terrible time to build because in the meantime the real estate market had taken a major dump.

It took about seven years to sell and we lost a bundle, and even half of that bundle was a killer. Besides all the renters we had to put in over the years, and the damage they did, and what the beach air does to a house on sand, the expenses kept on adding up. Suffice to say that recovering that loss was going to be just about impossible.

But let's back up. It's still 1993, and as I mentioned I'm paying a fortune for the LA Mexican house and somewhat less for the Arrowhead house. We decided to put the LA house on the market and four months later sold it.

For a major loss…

By now the word "loss"—notice it's a four-letter word—was now in my permanent vocabulary. The equity in the house was gone and we had to lay out our own money to pay off the loan.

Lake Arrowhead, here we come…

Lake Arrowhead:
We Came, We Saw, We Conquered … the Snow

It was June now, I'm out of work four months, and we have to move to the mountains. Thank God for that house, it turned out to be one of the best things we ever did, even though we were forced to do it.

The area is so beautiful, the air is so fresh, the house, a dream chalet, was comfortable and cozy. Maybe all our backing up financially wouldn't be so bad after all. The town has one movie house with four screens, and some decent restaurants. So all in all we started our new life again.

With a positive attitude to boot. Well, at least Toby as was positive. Me? I wanted a job. It wasn't happening, but we were okay. Toby took a decorating deal in a local store and seemed happy. I read a lot, listened to music, watched TV, and enjoyed the Lake Arrowhead Country Club. I wasn't totally broke, so in-between meetings and auditions I played golf three or four times a week, made some great friends in the Shores, the Speidels, the McGonigles, and a wonderful, giving character named Cam Alloway.

In November, we had our first snow, the first I'd seen since I left New York.

Also the last I wanted to see ...

Getting up and down the hill to LA for auditions became a test in courage. A single lane each way highway was all we had to get to the main road at the bottom to get to the freeway. Even stocking up at Costco was a chore.

We managed, but when you get what they call a "whiteout"—a nasty combination of fog and snow—you couldn't see two feet in front of you. I would test myself two to three times a week, out of necessity, to reach LA for the meetings and auditions.

Even though *Santa Barbara* was off the air in the states, it was still playing all over the world in early 1994, when the SB press department called and asked if Toby, Louise Sorel, my dear friend and co-star, and I would like to do a month of publicity in Europe.

Of course I said "no."

I was much too busy reading, watching TV, and playing golf. But I decided to give that all up for this four week, paid, first class vacation to meet—and greet—the fans in Europe.

It was a difficult decision to make, but I forced myself to go...

Back in the U.S.S.R.

Wow, what a trip! I felt like a king again. We were treated like royalty everywhere we went. Berlin, Tallin, Oslo, Helsinki, Stockholm, and Moscow. A dream trip if there ever was one.

In Europe, *Santa Barbara* was the number one show on television, and we were the next coming, messiah, whatever. What fun we had. Louise is even crazier than Toby, and between the two of them there was never a quiet moment—and a lot of laughs. There wasn't a city that "Lulu," or Louise, didn't leave something behind in the hotel room.

Usually her passport ...

Every place we went, security went with us to keep the crowds under control. It was absolutely so far removed from the states that I can't do justice in describing it. We were loved and idolized almost to the point of embarrassment.

Please, Spell the Name Right

Well, I never got to that point.

I loved it …

Four weeks later we were home and I was a bum again. Out of work and living on a mountaintop. But not for much longer.

Patriarch, Take Two

After about a month of being home I got a call from the producers at *Beverly Hills 90210*. They were looking for a man to play Steve's father, played by Ian Ziering on the show, who could also play golf.

Why golf? Because the first episode, I thought my only one, was with Barry Bonds and Stack Pierce, playing Bobby Bonds, who were having a match with Steve and me. "Rush," the character I was auditioning for, liked to cheat, and used a "hot" golf ball in the match.

Anyway I got the job, even though they forgot to ask if I played golf. They called me back an hour after I left the production office to show them I could swing a club. The thing is, I look great swinging, but in a game I stink.

It didn't matter; I had the job. Barry was a good guy and Stack an old friend, so the week went great and twenty-five episodes later, over four years, I was still around.

Boy's Club

I loved doing the show. Good boys all, Luke, Jason, and Ian, my son on the show, were great kids who seemed to genuinely enjoy having me around. I really had a fun four and a half years, in and out, not being a regular, that is. It was sad for me in my last year, especially when they didn't have me on the episode where my son Steve got married, and then snubbed me again when his wife on the show had a baby. That, I admit, did hurt a bit. I guess they had to save some money.

Who knows, who cares?

Me …

Sometimes life has a way of imitating art because, despite the fact that I played his father on television, when Ian Ziering married former dental hygienist and Playboy playmate Nikki Schieler on July 4th, 1997 his father wasn't invited. Well, at least not his TV father anyway. Maybe it was bad luck to snub the old man; after all, the two divorced several years later.

Unhappiness followed another of Ian's fellow *90210* alums when Jason Priestley was seriously injured in a practice run during a race at the Kentucky Speedway after his automobile crashed into a wall on August 11, 2002.

Like the rest of the country, I was shocked by the news and put in a call to Jason's publicist. I wasn't surprised when it wasn't returned. Jason had a lot of physical therapy to do and, I'm sure, a lot of calls to return. A good kid with a great heart, I'm sure I'm still on his "to do" list somewhere.

Luke Perry rounded out the trio in our "boys club," and I'm thrilled to say that his career has flourished since his *90210* days, doing star turns on cable in HBO's celebrated series *Oz* followed by his current stint in Showtime's breakaway hit *Jeremiah*.

A Girl Named Zelda

After *90210* was canceled, I got an offer to work on a comedy series based on ways to stay healthy. Yes, if it sounds odd it certainly was. Conventional thinking at the time was that, if it was funny enough, it could possibly be elaborated on and perhaps sold as a sitcom on cable TV.

The producers were doing twelve half-hour shows, shot in five weeks, so you can imagine the schedule it would entail. In sit-coms they usually rehearsed four days, then dress rehearsed and taped the fifth day in front of an audience.

What we were going to do was something not done before, and should never be done again.

I don't care *how* healthy you get.

The schedule I got would kill you anyway …

I was eventually hired, along with three other actors. Two of them were the most delightful people I've ever had the pleasure of working with. They were playing neighbors to me and the other actress playing my wife, who we'll just call "Zelda."

The younger couple, Sydney Andersen and Ray Young, were a joy and Sydney and I are still friends to this day. Sadly, Ray passed away several years ago. He was a dear, sweet, 6' 8" guy who you couldn't help but love.

Zelda was another story. A former star on Broadway, she was now somewhat older and, regrettably for aging women, having a tough time getting work. I have to think of Henny Youngman's old line, "Take my wife, please …" whenever dredging up my five weeks with Zelda.

Zelda was a devout Catholic, and a major talent, but had an evil streak that you could never see coming. She was sneaky bad; she should have become a ninja dressed in black, because that was her favorite color, and she wielded a wicked sword whenever using her mouth.

Dare you say a bad word and you'd hear about it. But the way she talked to the crew, was something else. Especially those from makeup and wardrobe. The worst situation I remember was the poker scene we were doing one day. Wardrobe and makeup were doing some last minute touching up as we were getting ready to shoot.

As they started she began screaming, "Get the fuck away from me! I've had enough of you two." The place went silent.

I looked at her and asked, "How the hell can you talk to them that way?"

She took a beat, looked up at me, and said, "Because it feels good."

I do not exaggerate; those were her exact words. That was just one of many instances that alienated everyone so badly that the wrap party, held on the last day of shooting, was put off two and a half hours until we knew Zelda would be on a plane for LA.

What a shame, and what a religious hypocrite.

By the way, the series didn't sell.

But Sydney, Ray, and I were healthier just because we'd met each other.…

The Russians Are Coming, The Russians Are Coming …

Months later I was shooting a French picture starring Christopher Lambert in Las Vegas. I was the only English speaking person other than the Vegas extras, and they didn't speak anyway. I received a call from a friend of a friend, Ed Fishman, who knew that *Santa Barbara* was still a major hit in Moscow.

Jed Allan

Turns out Chuck Norris was opening a gambling casino, which was one of about thirty at the time, called "Chuck Norris' Beverly Hills Casino." It just so happened that they needed several celebrity-types to appear, hang out, gamble, and have fun. For this they offered quite a decent amount of money.

So I'm thinking, "This is not too bad…"

I wrapped the French picture and a week later I'm on Delta airlines flight direct to Moscow. Now, as I mentioned, I'd already been there with Toby and Lulu, but this time I was flying solo and looking forward to meeting Norris and Ed when I arrived. As an added bonus, I soon found out that Lane Davies, who played my son on *Santa Barbara*, was going to be there. I'm getting happier by the minute.

This should be a fun trip…

It was all that and more. It was the beginning of a relationship with Moscow, St. Petersburg, and the wonderful but sometimes crazy Russians I was eventually to meet. It was also the first of at least six trips Ed and I made together in the next couple of years.

Chuck later found out that his investment was being ripped off and, within a year, had unceremoniously pulled his name off the sign above the casino—and tried to sue. A virtual impossibility in Russia.

It's very difficult to explain Moscow and the people. They are wonderful, can be charming, can be very illegal, and can drink … a lot! Aside from that, and being pathological liars, they were fairly normal. To classify liars you have to do business with them. Trust is not a word in the Russian dictionary.

As an example, Ed, myself, and several record people from New York and LA were invited to judge a beauty contest with women competing from all over Russia. I gotta tell you, that's a *lot* of women. And the beauty of some of them was something to behold.

Believe me when I tell you they *do* have teeth.

Anyway, we were scheduled for a two week trip to meet the 100 finalists and narrow them down to ten or fifteen, each of us asking different prepared questions and hoping for illuminating *unprepared* answers.

Please, Spell the Name Right

It was also a talent contest, much like a Russian version of the show *Star Search*. We took our jobs seriously, and worked hard to pick the final five of the fifteen women left after a few weeks, surprised to find that one was very average and, for the life of us, we couldn't find out how she'd gotten into the fifteen finalists.

Nice girl, but definitely the least of the entire group. Somehow she became the least of the final five. Well, we thought nothing about it and worked hard for the final days before the announcement. I remember that all the while this was going on TV crews for a Russia TV special were filming us and the girls, discussions with the girls, fights between the girls, and discussions amongst ourselves as we went through the entire process.

Everything seemed to be going fine except for the fact that nobody voted for this one girl and we felt terrible, since the competition was simply too tough for her. Yet despite what our votes said, she kept turning up like a bad penny.

Do I really have to tell you who won?

Turns out she was the niece of a Russian parliament member from St. Petersburg. That was the last beauty contest we judged. At least until Ed came up with a show called *Hollywood Star Time*, which he co-ventured with a Russian production company.

Of course, it was a steal from *Star Search*, but Ed had invested his own money and put on a big show and I got invited back again to be a judge on the panel. Surprise: Again it happened!

We voted, they picked the winner. Ed had no knowledge that the fix was in … again. The producers screwed him—and the other contestants—and they never made another show after the pilot.

So much for democracy in the "new" Russia …

"Na-Na" Never Again …

Six months after the *Hollywood Star Time* debacle, Ed gave me a call again and asked if I'd like another trip to Moscow. I said, "Oh no, not again, what for?"

He said, "There's a guy in Russia who's a friend of mine who says we

190

should look at this group called Na-Na." Ed went on to explain that this group of boys was described as somewhat like N-Sync or Backstreet Boys, Russian style. He was thinking of bringing them over, but as a trusted friend he wanted my opinion about the whole situation.

So I went back to Moscow yet again and saw their shows, and was surprised to find that they were actually five very talented young men. Now it wasn't just Ed who was thinking about bringing them back to the states. After all, I was in for ten percent just because I was around.

And so we did, carting "Na-Na" back to the states with us. It didn't cost us a dime, only our connections. Their manager paid for everything. They stayed for almost a year, off and on, eventually receiving a terrible offer from Arista records, which their manager didn't want. So off to Moscow they went and, last I heard, they were still performing all over the country.

Nice kids. I wish them well …

One night while in Moscow for a meeting with a producer for yet another TV series that also didn't work—as you can see we're having a rough time with the Russians by this point—Ed says to me, "I found a great nightclub you've got to see." By now I'm losing money in every casino in Moscow, so a nightclub was nice for a change.

We walked in past three armed guards standing under a sign that read, "Night Flight." The smoke was intolerable and all around me on all three levels of the club were hundreds of women dressed in all phases of undress, from beautiful and gorgeous to plug ugly. Not surprisingly the amount of men inside the crowded club, mostly Asians, was about fifteen percent.

I had never seen so many prostitutes gathered in one room in all my life…

But because I was CC Capwell, the patriarch of *Santa Barbara*, a hero to Muscovites and parts beyond, I was offered many freebies. Never partaking, I swear. The going rate was $350. Girls on the street got fifty dollars. Despite the tawdry nature of my first impression, I thought the club was interesting and different and it was what eventually made us try to put on a TV series about matchmaking called, "To Russia *for* Love."

Please, Spell the Name Right

We flew back to LA and immediately invested in a colleague named George Tricker, a wonderful writer and good friend who through the years had written many of the sitcoms I'd worked on. If the show was successful he would, in a sense, become a limited partner. Things were looking good.

Two months later we're back in Russia going on Aeroflot, the Russian equivalent of an old, large barn … with wings. To describe this plane would take all the verbosity I could muster. Suffice to say it smelled, there was no music, no TV, wires hanging loose, and flight attendants with heavy duty body odor. Twelve hours later, after much vodka and valium, we made it, never to fly Aeroflot again.

It was cheap, though…

This time in Moscow we had appointments with several TV studios and even the state owned station in Moscow. We were greeted royally; their thinking American money was coming in. We were looking for their money, of course, and in return would give them our talent as producer, director, star, and writer. After ten days and nights, many parties, and meeting many important Russians, we finally left for LA thinking we had a deal with a very well-known Russian producer.

So well-known I can't remember his name…

He "loved the concept" and consented to fly to LA to further discuss the project with our people and possible investors. We wanted to make a two-hour movie and either sell it as a Movie of the Week-slash-pilot or, barring that, try selling to cable and, as a last resort, go to video distribution to be able to protect the initial investment.

The Russian producer flew to LA to discuss final financing; we naturally paid his way. We, of course, thought we had a deal. He, of course, ate, drank, and lied for five days straight—and left promising us everything we asked for. The day he got on that plane to go home was the last time we ever saw or heard from him.

The Russians Are Going, The Russians Are Going …

2001:
Goodbye, Dearest One …

By 2001 my life was full of possibilities, for producing, working, playing golf, taking more vacations with Toby. The sky was the limit. In-between trips to Russia I completed a movie called *Carmen the Champion*, a boxing picture produced by the good folks at Trinity Broadcasting Network, a Christian organization.

Can you imagine a fight movie without one curse word?

I played the baddest of the bad guys—and enjoyed the hell out of it. It was well-written and directed by my good friend Lee Stanley, a wonderful guy with immense talent who should be very important in our business.

But when you're over fifty in our line of work … it's a bitch.

After I finished the picture I got a guest lead on *Walker: Texas Ranger*. It was a thrill to hook up with Chuck Norris again and, to my great delight, we renewed our connection with some good conversation and a great show. He surprised all of us by announcing that he and his wife of two years were expecting twins. Sixty and still going strong. Good for him. His life was beginning again.

Mine felt like it was over …

Three months later my wonder of wonders, the light I lived by, the dearest person I ever met, died. It was Thursday morning, and we were going to play golf for the first time together at seven-thirty a.m. She was taking lessons and loving it and I was so proud of her. I always was. I was awakened that morning by a strange breathing sound. I turned to look at my wife who it seemed was having a bad dream.

Please, Spell the Name Right

I said "Honey, wake up, wake up, you're having a bad dream, honey, wake up…"

Well, it wasn't a bad dream. She was in the middle of a grand mal seizure, and she was having difficulty breathing. I held her with one hand and dialed 911 with the other. When I got through the operator went down the list of things to do during a seizure—keep her airway open, try to calm her down—they tried to tell me what to do, the things you're supposed to know by now, but all I was doing was panicking, screaming over and over again, "Honey, please wake up."

She never did … she was having an aneurism. A very bad one.

Far from improving, her situation got worse. Though it seemed like seven years to me at the time, the paramedics got there in seven minutes. First they lost her, then they got her back. All the while I'm screaming in the background.

I just didn't know what to do …

We were in Oxnard on vacation at the time, so they took her to Oxnard Community Hospital. Before they did I somehow managed to call the kids. All I remember saying is, "Mom's sick, please come." I followed the ambulance in the police car, too upset to drive, and when I finally got there I was told "…it doesn't look good."

I totally fell apart. Friends from Oxnard got there right away and pretty soon my kids showed up, too. Trying to help them *and* myself was impossible, but before long the neurosurgeon and neurologist talked to me while Toby was lying in the emergency room. They showed me the CAT scan and other tests and explained that, for all intense and purposes, "she was gone." They said the brain damage from the aneurism was so severe that she'd never be able to make it without the respirator.

Emotions are indescribable at this moment. You'd rather die yourself than to have to make a life and death decision about someone you've spent forty-three years loving and worrying and carrying about. She was so special, bright, funny, caring, beautiful, loving, she was the most positive person I've ever met.

She walked into a room with her own special light. This is the woman I had to let go. The boys and I made the decision, held hands, and they disconnected her. She was gone in twenty seconds.

So was my life as I knew it…

She was buried two days later with 750 people coming to pay their respects. The phrase I heard most that day was the same as I had uttered when the doctor first gave me the grim news: "No, no it can't be, not Toby."

The next months were absolute hell. The pain was so intense I begged for help every day. I'd cry every night, screaming to myself, "No more pain, please, make it stop." A therapist told me "it will soften in time," but for those first six months or so I didn't believe it.

Then, one day, I said to myself, "This can't go on or I'll die." So I made several phone calls to friends in the business asking for help. One called me back. She was Julie Hanan-Caruthers, the executive producer of a daytime show called *Port Charles*. I owe her more thanks and love than I can express for getting me a job on that show. Not to mention a new lease on life. I was supposed to be on for just seven shows, and seven months later I was still playing Ed "the Angel."

Turns out *she* was the angel ...

The good people are there when you need them. Working was what I needed at that point to try to get my life started again. The pain will never leave, but the therapist I found was right: It *does* soften. The nightmares lessen, the crying lessens, you breathe a little better, you say, "Maybe I'll be okay."

Or, "At least I'll give it a good try."

It's taken awhile, but I'm working at being alive again ...

Be Patient, It's Almost Over ...

After seven months in LA doing the show, going to bonding groups that didn't bond in LA and Encino, I decided to come home and try to live my life without Toby. You have to start someplace, and home was it. I had to be alone to live alone.

I was fortunately introduced to a guy named Larry Spellman who was a personal manager—Jerry Vale, Frank Gorshin, Al Martino, etc.—and a man who had lost his wife two months before Toby. He also wasn't doing well. The two of us were able to talk, and break bread, and go to movies, and talk some more. His love for his wife CeeCee, was no less than mine for Toby. This bonding became a terrific friendship and one we still, when needed, share.

After being home for two months I received a call from Ed Fishman about Russia again. I said, "You can't be serious."

Ed was proposing yet another trip over to Russia, to St. Petersburg this time, where a mayoral candidate there wanted us to "stump" for him, going out on his political fundraisers and "speaking to the people" about him on his behalf. It wasn't exactly Shakespeare, but when I heard the fee they were offering it wasn't exactly Much Ado About Nothing either.

So Ed and I flew back to Russia with a stopover in Frankfurt and had just settled into our hotel rooms, about to discuss strategy for meeting with the candidate to be the next mayor of St. Petersburg, when Ed got a phone call.

His ninety-three-year-old mother had just died …

The time difference between Frankfurt to LA is about eleven hours, and by now funeral preparations were already being made. Ed felt horribly guilty for being away when his mother passed, and had already booked a flight to go back home and be in attendance at the funeral. Certainly, I understood, and was ready to make my own return flight.

But Ed disagreed. He told me the mayoral candidate was a real charmer, already understood the situation, and would be expecting me the next morning. I was shocked, and saddened over Ed's mother, but I couldn't be much help to him anyway so I decided to stay and finish the job.

I met with the mayoral candidate, whose name now escapes me, as if I could have ever pronounced it in the first place, but as Ed had pre-warned me he was a jovial fellow and took to me right off. I kissed him on both cheeks as I got off the plane, as if I actually knew the man. TV cameras and crowds had gathered at St. Petersburg airport and the first meeting when off like clockwork.

Jed Allan

The campaign was a blur, and mostly I remember trying to convince many staring crowds of grim babushkas (or Russian peasants) how terrific Mr. So and So was, and they had no idea what I was talking about. Why? Because the wanna-be mayor, who spoke good English, neglected to hire a translator. So there I was, stumping for this mayor whom I'd only just met, telling a crowd of hungry peasants how great this guy was, and what does he do?

He repeats my words in Russian, telling them how great he was!

Stupid, is a better word ...

Needless to say, despite the fact that I was more popular than the current mayor of St. Petersburg, the campaign wasn't going over too well. So much so that the candidate, who nonetheless seemed to be thoroughly enjoying the experience, let me go home a day early. "Fine with me," I thought. "My check's already cleared ..."

As I sat in my hotel room that night, making arrangements to leave a day early, I got a call from Ed's personal secretary, who sounded flustered as she exclaimed, "Whatever you do, don't call Ed."

"Why not?" I asked her, puzzled by her cryptic request. "What's wrong?"

She explained that Ed's beloved son "Bo" had committed suicide, shooting himself in the head behind his bedroom door after talking to his girlfriend. He had been young, about to turn twenty-one the very next day, as a matter of fact, and his parents had heard the shotgun blast. They'd been downstairs, with Ed's wife, Jane, reaching him first. There was absolutely nothing they could do.

She's never been quite the same since.

Nor has Ed ...

It's amazing how your life can change in an instant.

As I loitered in a bookstore in St. Petersburg airport awaiting my flight back home to the states, I picked up an *International Newsweek* and in it was a story about the death of a mayoral candidate in ...St. Petersburg.

Reading further, I was relieved to find out that it wasn't *my* mayoral candidate, but the news was nonetheless chilling. Conventional wisdom pointed to the incumbent mayor as the key, since he had his connections to major government people. This was what *International Newsweek* was intimating. Luckily, my campaign speeches hadn't exactly helped out my guy, so he wasn't considered a threat.

Turns out he only got two percent of the vote come Election Day.

It was the first time I was ever happy I'd failed at a job so miserably.

Just think what might have happened to him if I'd been a hit!

Nonetheless, as I stood there in the airport reading about political intrigue and thinking how little I knew about the man I was stumping for, I couldn't help but wonder if there were hired assassins tailing me from the bookstore back to my gate.

I was never so glad to be on a plane in my life, despite the empty house that awaited me back in California, and once on the plane I wasted no time in re-introducing myself to those constant companions who had accompanied me on other trips to Russia: Vodka and valium.

Never to go back to Russia again. I just wanted to go home. I just wanted my world to feel good again. It was getting better every day; I knew it, I felt it, I liked the feeling.

Epilogue:
The Kids Are All Right

The 90s are gone and 2000 came and went. It's been over two years since losing my beautiful Toby, and maybe it's finally getting easier, at least I can smile a little more and I can wake up and get out of bed. Thank God for my family, my friends, and the new joys in my life. Somehow, with help, you find a way to go on.

When the help comes in the form of a new relationship, a personal, loving caring one, you grab on and hold it tight. Experience it. Enjoy it. I'm finally doing that.

These days, I'm in the midst of a new show, and things are looking up again. The horizons are getting closer, there's work out there for me. I'm even going back to singing again. Work is starting to come in, a different kind of work than I've been offered in the past.

In fact, when the folks at *CSI: Miami* offered me the role of a palsied senior citizen, I didn't flinch. Cause I am a senior citizen. I forget sometimes. I saw an opportunity to make him more multi-dimensional, and even requested my character sit in a wheelchair. Who knows, maybe I'm even finally becoming that most sought after type: A character actor.

If I lost my hair and got fat I might work a lot more.

There's something to think about …

What else is funny to think about is the new show I'm doing, which happens to be *General Hospital*, in which I play Edward Quartermaine. The old, old, *old* patriarch. But the funniest part about it is the guy who plays my son, Stuart Damon, is exactly my age. If they can bring people back from the dead three times over on daytime drama, I think I can make this work.

My guys are men now. Mitch became an actor all over again, this time in sales, and is doing beautifully. He was married, and divorced, and has two beautiful children, Jake and Kaytie, who I adore and who he dotes on. He's now starting a soap opera of his own; you wouldn't believe it if I told you.

Rick is now thirty-seven, and also in the business, but on the other side. He started out as an editor, and later went into post-production, and is now a tele cine colorist who lives in San Fernando Valley with his wife Kristi. If something has to be done in our family, Rick's the "go to" guy. Mr. Steady has his own two beauties named Rachel and Hannah, Hannah being named after Toby; her full name is Hannah Toby Brown. Isn't that beautiful?

Someday, maybe, we'll call her Toby Two!

And my former "wild child," Dean, the one who gave me gray hair a dozen years too early? He's long since changed his ways and is on the other side of the law now: He's become a lawyer. Married to his beautiful wife, Meryl, their two gorgeous kids are named Alexis and Nick.

Though the guys had been a handful growing up, they've each and every one of them become men I'm proud to call my own. Many actors' kids grow up spoiled rotten, but not my three boys. I'd like to say I had a hand in that and, while I was around more than most, I have to give all the credit to my Toby.

Toby was the one who put her indelible mark on the signature of her boys' lives. They got all their great values and the love and the giving and the caring from both of us, but she was the captain of the ship.

She was the lynchpin of the family and if they didn't have her, well, I just know there would have been another kind of life awaiting them on the other side of adulthood.

I couldn't do what she had to do, the patience and the positive cheerleading and the spirit and the love of life she gave to them. She had all of that—in spades—and that's what made them what they are today.

I'm pretty sure my boys would agree …

Jed Allan

If I ever had any doubts that Toby and I did okay with our children the following fortieth anniversary card from my son Dean was all that was needed. Enjoy:

Mom and Dad,

You have always given us all that we could ask for. Love, affection, laugher, joy, and aspersions of greatness. You never said we couldn't; we always could. I remember that always.

Now that I'm an adult, I still hear from both of you. I learned that after forty years of marriage two people can still have such love and affection for each other, period, that there is so much laughter and joy, and no matter how much time has transpired, in fact it seems that time makes the joy deeper, the laughter louder, the affection more soothing, and the love more intense.

I look forward to the passing of time with my wife, because I've seen how wonderful it has been for both of you. The last thing I want to leave you with, is to remember the aspirations of greatness. You have achieved greatness for the last forty years, there's a lot more to come, a lot more to aspire to. I love you both with every ounce of my soul …

Your son,

Dean

I'd say we did just fine …